GOVERNMENT AT WORK

GOVERNMENT AT WORK
Best Practices and Model Programs

Marc Holzer
Kathe Callahan

SAGE Publications
International Educational and Professional Publisher
Thousand Oaks   London   New Delhi

For information:

SAGE Publications, Inc.
2455 Teller Road
Thousand Oaks, California 91320
E-mail: order@sagepub.com

SAGE Publications Ltd.
6 Bonhill Street
London EC2A 4PU
United Kingdom

SAGE Publications India Pvt. Ltd.
M-32 Market
Greater Kailash I
New Delhi 110 048 India

Printed in the United States of America

Library of Congress Cataloging-in-Publication Data

Holzer, Marc.
  In defense of the public service: exemplary government / by Marc Holzer and Kathe Callahan.
    p. cm.
  Includes bibliographical references (p.) and index.
  ISBN 0-7619-0240-6 (cloth : acid-free paper). — ISBN 0-7619-0241-4 (pbk. : acid-free paper)
  1. Government productivity—United States. I. Callahan, Kathe. II. Title.
  JK768.4.H65 1997
  353.3'0973—dc21   97-21078

97 98 99 00 01 02 03 10 9 8 7 6 5 4 3 2 1

Acquiring Editor:	Catherine Rossbach
Editorial Assistant:	Kathleen Derby
Production Editor:	Michèle Lingre
Production Assistant:	Lynn Miyata
Typesetter/Designer:	Danielle Dillahunt
Indexer:	Julie Grayson
Cover Designer:	Candice Harman
Print Buyer:	Anna Chin

To
Ben and Matt
Dan and Emily

Contents

Preface

———■

The impetus for this book is our frustration that although the public sector is a productive, necessary, and important part of our society, it does little to provide evidence that might counter the stereotyped arguments of government's critics.

There is a small literature, chief among which are Goodsell's *The Case for Bureaucracy* and Osborne's and Gaebler's *Reinventing Government*. We certainly share Goodsell's (1993) "growing irritation with a view that has long been dominant in popular culture and the social sciences, namely that governmental bureaucracy in the United States is a generalized failure and threat" (p. ix). Goodsell is taking issue with the popular assumptions of incompetence in government, as did Herbert Kaufman (1981), who observed earlier that, "more and more people are apparently convinced that bureaucracy is whirling out of control and are both infuriated and terrified by the prospect . . . [but] the epidemic is more rhetoric than substance" (p. 1).

By presenting evidence of competency and productivity, we hope that this book will help begin to reverse the negative, distorted stereotypes that are deeply imprinted in the public consciousness. We argue that public servants are productive, successful, and professional. By no means is the public sector "dead in the water." Negative images do not withstand careful scrutiny: Government does a good job, often an outstanding job, in difficult circumstances. Throughout, we present evidence that public servants do their jobs surprisingly well and deliver a "basket" of critical services, despite the constant barrage of negative images, superficial criticism, and minimal public support. By using cases from the Exemplary State and Local (EXSL) Awards Program, sponsored by the National Center for Public Productivity (NCPP), we describe how the best public organizations have developed systematic problem-solving strategies and have demonstrated a remarkable capacity to be innovative. By delineating imaginative approaches to capacity building by public servants and public organizations, we hope to construct an agenda by which governments might develop even greater problem-solving capacities.

Our intended audience is multifaceted. We expect public managers will find our evidence useful in defending their profession, in explaining why they are professional public servants rather than stereotypical "bureaucrats," and in approaching innovation on a more open basis. A parallel audience is the set of policymakers—elected officials, the media, and interest groups—whose propensities toward "bureaucrat bashing" might be mitigated by our arguments. Thus, the innovations we describe may help accelerate the problem-solving dialogue between external critics and appointed officials, moving beyond gamesmanship to real change.

We also hope to pique the imagination of our academic colleagues in public administration, political science, management, and other related fields by suggesting that they have not yet recognized the full extent of public sector problem solving. This book is also intended to capture the imagination of present and future students in the field, with the objective of drawing more of the best and brightest to government service as society's most challenging service. And we hope to attract the attention of government's corporate critics, some of whom might approach temporary public service with a more balanced attitude.

References

Goodsell, C. (1993). *The case for bureaucracy* (2nd ed.). Chatham, NJ: Chatham House.
Kaufman, H. (1981). Fear of bureaucracy: A raging pandemic. *Public Administration Review,* 41(1), 1-9.
Osborne, D., & Gaebler, T. (1992). *Reinventing government.* Reading, MA: Addison-Wesley.

Acknowledgments

———————————————————————■

We would like to acknowledge the dedicated public servants whose stories we tell. These individuals strive with sincerity and compassion to provide exemplary services to the people they serve. Their efforts and accomplishments provided the inspiration for this book. We are especially appreciative of those public servants who took the additional initiative of applying for Exemplary State and Local Awards so that their problem-solving strategies might be shared as models for other, equally dedicated colleagues throughout the public sector.

We are especially indebted to our academic colleagues and the Sage editorial team members who so incisively evaluated this work: Evan Berman, Meredith Newman, Dorothy Olshfski, and Vatche Gabrielian. They suggested valuable modifications and additions. And the project came to a successful conclusion only with the advice and detailed attention of the Sage Publications editorial team: Catherine Rossbach, Kris Bergstad, Kathleen Derby, Michèle Lingre, and many others.

Our families provided patient support, and in addition to our children—to whom this book is dedicated—it is our spouses, Mady and Neil, to whom we are particularly indebted.

1

GOVERNMENT AS PROBLEM SOLVER

■
PUBLIC SERVICE AS COMMITTED SERVICE

Despite negative images, low pay, and adverse circumstances, many people do choose to serve their fellow citizens in the spirit of the oath to public service first sworn by citizens of ancient Athens:

> *We will strive unceasingly to quicken*
> *the public sense of public duty;*
> *That thus . . . we will transmit this city*
> *not only not less, but greater, better and more beautiful*
> *than it was transmitted to us.*
>
> The Athenian Oath

Today, the Athenian Oath is inscribed at the Maxwell School of Citizenship and Public Affairs of Syracuse University. Many public servants are responding to such values, abstractions, or callings to serve others, to solve challenging problems, to improve the public welfare. They are dedicated to their clients. They put in long hours and work under difficult conditions. Although their accomplishments are usually not considered newsworthy, those who have received formal recognition suggest a depth of commitment to the public service that the public rarely recognizes:

> A recent Sloan Foundation Public Service Award recipient was Ed Wagner, an Assistant Commissioner of Environmental Protection in New York City, whose administration of the city's massive wastewater treatment and disposal system saved hundreds of millions of dollars. ("Six Bright Stars," 1990, p. 1)

> The American Society for Public Administration honored Carol M. Fay, District Director for the Internal Revenue Service in Salt Lake City, for her leadership abilities and self motivation which had a significant impact on increased program effectiveness, the public image of the IRS, employee morale and agency productivity. (American Society for Public Administration, National Public Service Award, 1993, p. 5)

> The National Academy of Public Administration designated Gordon M. Sherman, Commissioner of Social Security's Atlanta Region, as a National Public Service Award Winner for instituting innovations that significantly increased productivity while saving taxpayers money. (National Academy of Public Administration, National Public Service Award, 1990)

Wagner, Fay, and Sherman typify the sense of commitment that quietly pervades government. Most public employees are not commissioners or directors, but work "hands on" to improve the quality of our lives. They teach our children, assure our safety, distribute social benefits, rehabilitate the disabled, drive our buses and trains, fix our roads, deliver the mail, defend our national interests, and monitor the quality of our water and buildings. As teachers and social workers, police and military personnel, members of the fire service and of emergency services, they often do so for intangible rewards. According to the Public Employees Roundtable, they place "a high value on commitment to public service and the rewards of seeing the consequences of one's efforts."

Social Worker Mary Virginia Douglass underscores that commitment:

> We don't have plush office space like corporate America. For many years we weren't treated like professionals, but this office is very professional. . . . We have to take everybody who comes here. Unlike private agencies, we cannot pick and choose our clientele. You've got to love it to stay. . . . I've been here 25 years. (Reeves, 1989, p. 22)

Teacher Lynn Borg is typical of corporate executives who are willing to make less in the public sector:

> It occurred to me one day that whether I saved the company several thousand dollars or hired 10 people tomorrow it wouldn't make a difference. Some people feel they were put here for a reason, and I guess I feel like that . . . This was the best thing I ever did. I wake up in the morning, and I can't wait to get there. (Smetanka, 1990, p. 1)

Thomas Downs (1988), who has headed several large public organizations, makes the argument for public service particularly compelling:

> Only in public service can you find the sense of completion that comes from working on a successful program—to reduce infant mortality, for example, and then realizing that 35 more children are alive this year as a result of that effort. Only in public service can you participate in a process that helps move individuals from mental hospitals back in to the community. The opportunity to help solve a community problem and then to witness the changes that occur is the cement that binds us to public service . . . Public service is about babies living, fires being extinguished, garbage collected, crimes solved, people moved. (pp. 7-8)

INDIVIDUAL DIFFERENCES IN
THE PUBLIC AND PRIVATE SECTORS

As Douglass, Borg, Downs, and thousands of other public servants typify, people who choose careers in the public sector are atypical. They are dedicated to serving their fellow citizens and are motivated by the desire in some small way to make this world a better place to live. Public servants often make less money than their private sector counterparts, and many work in environments that challenge even the most optimistic, creative, and industrious personalities. What makes these people so different and what makes them want to serve the public?

The literature indicates that there is a significant difference in the characteristics of people who work in the public sector compared to those employed in the private sector. Wittmer (1991) cites numerous studies that indicate work-related values, reward preferences, needs, and personality types vary significantly between the sectors. Individuals in government organizations are different, in important respects, from those in private organizations. Because of self-selection, socialization, or other factors, public sector employees care more about serving the public (Rainey, 1991).

In a comparative study of professional values, Nalbandian and Edwards (1983) found that although private and public administrators shared a common administrative orientation, private sector administrators place a higher value on efficiency, while public administrators valued the public interest to a much greater degree.

Cacioppe and Mock (1984) found that people working in public organizations were motivated more by factors such as providing a service or product that helps other people, or by self-development and self-fulfillment, than people who work in the private sector. Those in private organizations were motivated more by extrinsic factors, such as money. Their study concludes that certain personality types are attracted to the public sector. That is, many public managers are more concerned about social welfare, education, unemployment, and equity than are their profit-making private counterparts.

Rainey, Backoff, and Levine (1976), in their comparative essay of the public and private sectors, cited individual differences regarding incentives and values. Public sector employees are motivated, to a greater degree than private sector employees, by intrinsic rewards such as helping others, doing something meaningful, "power and glory." Conversely, private sector employees are motivated by extrinsic rewards such as money and other material incentives. A 1982 survey by Rainey of 275 public and private managers found statistically significant differences on the importance of pay and of performing meaningful public service.

Wittmer (1991) concludes that public sector managers and employees differ from their private sector counterparts in terms of work-related values, reward preferences, needs, and personality types. Managers in government agencies that have both profitability and public policy objectives (such as toll roads, lottery agencies, and summons-issuing units of public safety organizations) are faced with conflicting objectives.

> There is some evidence that managers . . . develop a form of "organizational cognitive dissonance." . . . This appears to be particularly problematic when government "instructions" on social objectives are vague, conflicting, changing, or implicit. It appears that many joint enterprises resolve the dissonance by concluding that profitability is not important. (Brooks, 1987, p. 36)

In spite of the conflicting objectives, it is encouraging that social objectives are the dominant objectives.

WHY IS THE PUBLIC SECTOR DIFFERENT?

Perhaps the most critical distinction between public and private administration is that public administration is deeply rooted in public law (Moe & Gilmour, 1995). Public law, in an ideal world, provides the framework for the process and procedures of governmental organization and management.

The ideal of American democracy assumes a special relationship between public servants and the citizens they serve. The assumption is that all public administrators will function within, and be guided by, the moral truths found in our Constitution. As Woodrow Wilson (1887) wrote: "Liberty cannot live apart from constitutional principle; and no administration, however perfect and liberal its methods, can give men more than a poor counterfeit of liberty if it rests upon illiberal principles of government" (p. 198).

Broad constitutional values, robust individual civil rights and liberties, integrity, and due process (Rosenbloom & Carroll, 1990) should guide public administrators as they serve the public. However, constitutional values often conflict and frequently run counter to the values embodied in private sector management. Although efforts to serve the public more efficiently and cost-effectively tout "efficient" private sector management techniques, the constitutional values of equity, fairness, and due process are often compromised when such techniques are introduced.

According to Rosenbloom (1993), sovereignty, which is the concept of supreme political power and authority, resides in the people, who exercise it through a representative government. Public administration and public service are consequently considered a "public trust." As representatives of the sovereign, public administrators face situations that are considerably different than those faced by private sector administrators.

> Public administrators are engaged in the formulation and implementation of policies that allocate resources, values and status in a fashion that is binding on the society as a whole. Their actions embody the will of the sovereign, which means that the actions of public administrators have the

force of law and the coercive power of the government behind them. (Rosenbloom, 1993, p. 11)

The distinctive character of the public sector is illustrated by its foundation in public law, its responsiveness to a "higher purpose," its sovereign role, its determination to see that constitutional rights are protected, its position of placing the public interest before personal gain, and its special relationship between the public servants and the citizens they serve.

Frederickson and Hart (1985) ponder the moral obligations of American public administrators and define what they view as the special relationship between the public servant and the citizens he or she serves as the "patriotism of benevolence":

> We define the primary moral obligation of the public service in this nation as the patriotism of benevolence: an extensive love of all people within our political boundaries and the imperative that they must be protected in all of the basic rights granted to them by the enabling documents. If we do not love others, why should we work to guarantee the regime values to others? . . . The special relationship that must exist between public servants and citizens in a democracy is founded upon the conscious knowledge about the citizens that they are loved by the bureaucracy. . . . The primary duty of the public servants is to be the guardians and guarantors of the regime values for the American public. (pp. 549, 551)

Thus, a century of considered dialogue concludes that the public and private sectors are different. Public law and constitutional values frame the process and procedures of government agencies and management. The multiple, diverse, and contradictory expectations of the public sector create a complex working environment that is unequaled in the private sector, in other words, the "patriotism of benevolence" attracts to the public sector individuals who are driven by a desire to serve the public good.

GOVERNMENT AS NECESSARY

According to Siedman (1984), "the American public's love-hate relationship with its government produces demands for services, assistance, and protection while denigrating the people, processes, and costs necessary to meet those demands" (p. 4). From the outside, government appears to be the "problem," an argument politicians use to great advantage as they bemoan "large government" and berate the growth of public spending. But viewed from the inside, the services, the accomplishments, the problems solved that Downs (1988) cites are only some of those that society demands from its public servants. Government is a necessary, productive sector, providing important, critical services that meet society's needs, services we take for granted: Our mail is delivered, our garbage collected, our streets protected, and our children educated.

Some services are appropriate only to government. Public safety, public health, and public highways are necessary to the very existence of our society. Just as the armed services have replaced the private armies of feudal eras, today police, criminal justice, and fire and emergency services are virtually all publicly funded, publicly operated, and publicly controlled. We assume our streets and highways must be public, that our parks must be open to all our citizens, and that our public schools will educate all applicants. As protector of our common assets, such as water and air, public sector water systems have replaced polluted private wells, public sector sewage systems have superseded polluting septic systems, and public sector regulations have sharply decreased air pollution. As protector of our rights, government is the locus for programs of affirmative action, human rights, and legal protections for individuals and businesses. Our society simply could not function without a wide range of public services.

Some services are problem-solving systems of last resort, missions at which other sectors of our society have failed. In these instances, government is charged with solving unpleasant or unprofitable societal problems that the private sector (despite arguments for privatization) has turned away from or abandoned as unprofitable. Our society has high expectations that public servants will "solve" such difficult problems as the following.

Transportation. Although New York City's subways were built early in the 20th century as competing profit-making concerns, by 1950 the city was forced to take them over. Other cities and states had no choice but to operate the commuter railroads, some of which dated to the mid-1800s. By the 1970s, the federal government had taken over virtually all of the then-unprofitable long-haul railroads under the umbrella of AMTRAK; states and local governments have recycled abandoned rights-of-way for recreational purposes.

Housing. Unprofitable, privately built housing, almost always in poor condition and in poor neighborhoods, becomes the responsibility of government when landlords default. Millions of people who can no longer afford privately owned housing are sheltered in publicly built projects, shelters, and subsidized housing because the private market no longer finds it profitable to provide rental alternatives. New York City, Chicago, Los Angeles, and other large cities have tens of thousands of such units or apartments. With the failure of hundreds of privately owned savings and loan associations, the federal government's Resolution Trust Corporation also had to take over tens of thousands of homes and office buildings.

Health Care. For tens of millions of our citizens, the only access to health care is through government-funded clinics and hospitals, or public payments to private providers. Private hospitals routinely point poor patients toward public sector alternatives. Immunization records are checked by the public schools, which are an important link in ensuring that virtually all children become immunized even if their parents have been negligent. The public health is protected by agencies that systematically work to suppress such diseases as TB and to prevent a wide range of infectious behaviors. Addicts who suffer from drug-related illness most often turn to public clinics and hospital emergency rooms. Public sector health organizations are the first lines of defense against the drug-related and AIDS-related illnesses that are overwhelming our public health and hospital systems.

By default, public assumption of private responsibilities continues over the full spectrum of our society's services. Government agencies run thousands of other enterprises that were once private but are now public or publicly subsidized, such as colleges and universities, airports, terminals, wholesale markets, theaters, and parks. When private outputs become public problems, government is called upon to compensate for those unanticipated or unpleasant consequences. If toxic industrial waste leaches out of landfills or pollutes our air, we turn to government to clean up the problems of poisoned waters and acid rain. If manufacturing workers are displaced as plants close and move to areas of lower labor costs, those workers become public responsibilities—for unemployment and retraining in the short term, and often for health care and financial support in the long term. If individuals violate the law, they often become the long-term responsibility of the criminal justice system.

Some public services are simply cost-effective bargains. They are affordable, and therefore more accessible, alternatives to comparable private services. The most successful case may be higher education. As against private colleges, which can cost $20,000 or more a year for tuition, public institutions of higher education typically charge no more than half that and often much less (although the full cost of each is higher: Public institution are usually subsidized and private institutions are also supported by gifts and endowments). In one suburban county, for example, tuition at a private institutions is $23,000, as against as little as $2,600 at a public counterpart. New York's City University charged no tuition until 1976, yet its City College has produced more Nobel Prize winners than any private institution, including members of the Ivy League. More than 60% of America's (54) Nobel laureates in medicine and physiology were financially supported by government in their prize-winning careers (Public Employees Roundtable, n.d.).

Mass transit is often much cheaper and more widely available than private express buses and taxis. Even the much criticized postal service is a bargain, delivering a 2-day priority package for only $3, anywhere in the country, while U.P.S. or Federal Express charge from $6 to $12 for the same service; the postal service's first class mail rate of 32 cents is a worldwide bargain.

We take good government for granted. The services cited above are visible and familiar. Many others are as necessary, but virtually invisible. Public servants quietly provide many of the critical linkages a complex society requires. As regulators, they oversee the fiscal health of our banks and the quality of much of our food. As arbitrators they attempt to settle disputes before they enter the court system. As mechanics and engineers they safely maintain our basic systems of water supply and sewage. As extension agents they help our farmers be more productive. As lab workers and statisticians they help determine the causes of mysterious epidemics. As technicians they monitor the quality of our air and water. There are thousands of such jobs.

TYPICAL FAMILIES

Public services are not produced for some amorphous "society." As individuals and families we have seemingly insatiable appetites for the services that public servants provide. In the course of a single day members of a typical family will routinely go about their business without thinking of the *public* services that make that possible, services that they take for granted.

Family A lives in a large city and has three children, all born in public hospitals and who attend public schools. Both parents commute to work on public transit. Although they live in a private building, their rent is federally subsidized because their income is just above the official poverty line. They borrow books from a public library and ask questions of a public safety officer.

Family B lives in the suburbs and consists of a single mother with a daughter of preschool age. The mother drives to work over public highways and has enrolled her daughter in a government-subsidized day care center. Two evenings a week the mother is herself enrolled in a degree program at the county's community college.

Family C is considered affluent and lives on a farm. The family consists of two parents and five children. Their crops are federally subsidized. One of their parents is maintained in a nursing home by Medicaid and Social Security payments, and one of their children, who has been diagnosed with a serious learning disability, receives extensive tutoring and counseling services from the local school district.

SUCCESSES ARE ROUTINE

Despite the stereotypes and the broad range of services that we call upon its members to provide, the public sector is often innovative, entrepreneurial, and savvy—using state-of-the-art methods to improve efficiency and quality, to achieve outcomes as promised. As Osborne and Gaebler (1992) conclude in *Reinventing Government,*

> We were astounded by the degree of change taking place . . . . Public sector institutions—from state and local governments to school districts to the Pentagon—are transforming the bureaucratic models they have inherited from the past, making government more flexible, creative, and entrepreneurial. (p. xxii)

We agree with their findings, but we are not astounded. There has been, and continues to be, a great deal of work within the public management community as to how to improve the processes of service delivery. There are many examples of innovation within the public sector, many productive applications of knowledge, many confirmations of more efficient and higher-quality services. *Reinventing Government* is just one of the latest rediscoveries of that work. As Poister (1988) concludes,

> Despite the negative perceptions of the public bureaucracy that prevail in some quarters, successes are routinely scored by administrative agencies at all levels of government. These range from single episodes of satisfactory interactions with individual clients to the effective implementation of new programs and the development of innovative policies, strategies and treatments. (pp. 27-28)

At the state level, for example, New York State's Management and Productivity Program has saved more than one billion dollars since 1982, $200 million in 1995 alone. Recent initiatives have accomplished the following:

- Produced substantial recurring savings, particularly in the areas of welfare, Medicaid, and reductions of administrative burdens on agencies.
- Encouraged employee involvement in efforts to save funds and improve services.
- Enhanced accountability for the effective operation of state programs.
- Assisted local governments through a variety of technical assistance and savings projects.
- Applied new information systems and energy conservation technologies to reduce costs and improve services.

At the county level, Streib and Waugh (1991) have found considerable confidence in the administrative and political capacities of counties to design, implement, finance, and manage effective programs. For example, Los Angeles County's Productivity Improvement Program achieved millions of dollars in savings and national recognition (Carr, 1991; Dobbs, 1992). The program was driven by management support, employee participation and recognition, open communication, financial incentives, and networking. It was evidence of commitments to the goals of efficiency, effectiveness, and responsiveness.

At the local level, Ammons (1991) identified 35 jurisdictions and 39 officials as reputational leaders in local government productivity and innovation. The Local Government Information Network (LOGIN; n.d.) contains a database of more than 50,000 cases of innovative, entrepreneurial accomplishment at the state, county, and municipal levels.

Hard evidence that "government works" can be found in state, county, and municipal awards programs. Each year, thousands of projects are nominated for formal recognition by associations of their peers (see Exhibit 1.1), such as the National League of Cities, the U.S. Conference

of Mayors, the American Society for Public Administration, the League
of California Cities, and the International Personnel Management Association. After rigorous, objective scrutiny, hundreds receive awards as
models of problem solving and revitalization. They have accomplished
what government's critics demand: entrepreneurial actions by public
servants to improve public services and save public tax dollars. Those
successes in federal, state, and local agencies are directly counter to
assumptions that public servants care little about operational efficiency
and effectiveness. *(text continued on page 19)*

EXHIBIT 1.1
PUBLIC SECTOR AWARDS PROGRAMS

The *Exemplary State and Local Awards Program (EXSL),* sponsored by
the National Center for Public Productivity (NCPP), is designed to
encourage productivity, creativity, and innovations in state and local
government. This nationwide program, established in 1989, recognizes public initiatives that are designed to improve the quality of
government services and operations. Winning programs serve as
models of best practices for other states and municipalities that are
trying to improve the quality of their government services and operations. Award winners are recognized nationally through a series of
publications produced by the NCPP.
  For further information contact:

> The National Center for Public Productivity
> Rutgers University
> Graduate Department of Public Administration
> 360 King Boulevard
> Hill Hall 701
> Newark, NJ 07102
> Phone: (973) 353-5504/1531 extension 28 or 23
> Fax: (973) 353-5907
> E-mail: ncpp@andromeda.rutgers.edu
> http://newark.rutgers.edu/~ncpp/

The *Innovations in American Government Awards: A Program of the
Ford Foundation and the John F. Kennedy School of Government at
Harvard University* strives to identify and celebrate outstanding exam-
ples of creative problem solving in the public sector. Since the Inno-

vations Program's inception in 1986, it has recognized 180 innovative programs, which have received $12 million in Ford Foundation grants. In 1995, eligibility was expanded from innovations in state and local government to encompass innovations in federal government as well. Though the program encompasses all levels of American government, it retains its historic focus on domestic programs. The Innovations in American Government awards are intended to draw attention to exemplary achievements in government problem solving and to amplify the voices of public innovators in communicating their practices. In addition, the Kennedy School develops instructional materials based on the contributions of award-winning innovations to the art of creative problem solving in the public sector.

For further information contact:

> Innovations in American Government
> Taubman Center for State and Local Government
> John F. Kennedy School of Government
> Harvard University
> 79 J.F.K. Street
> Cambridge, MA 02138
> Phone: (617) 495-0558
> E-mail: http://ksgwww.harvard.edu/innovat/

The *All-America City Award Program (AAC),* sponsored by the National Civic League, is the nation's oldest and most renowned community recognition award. Ten communities a year are honored for effectively addressing their most critical challenges through the collaborative efforts of citizens, nonprofit organizations, government, businesses, and community-based groups. All-America cities and communities have confronted some of the nation's most pressing social problems, including crime, substance abuse, economic development, environmental protection, education, health care, housing, and race relations. The award winners exemplify the philosophy of "self-government" advocated by National Civic League founder Theodore Roosevelt—the notion that every individual and every sector must take responsibility for the entire community.

For further information contact:

> The National Civic League
> 1445 Market Street, Suite 300
> Denver, CO 80202-1728
> Phone: (303) 571-4404
> E-mail: ncl@csn.net

The *American Society for Public Administration (ASPA),* established in 1939, is the largest and most prominent professional association in the field of public administration. With a diverse membership of more than 12,000 practitioners, teachers, and students, ASPA has emerged as the focal point for intellectual and professional interaction, thereby serving as the principal arena for linking thought and practice within the field of public administration. Various sections and chapters of ASPA sponsor award programs.
For further information contact:

The American Society for Public Administration
1120 G Street, NW, Suite 700
Washington, D.C. 20005
Phone: (202) 393-7878
Fax: (202) 638-4952
E-mail: http://www.aspanet.org

The *Hammer Award,* sponsored by the National Performance Review (NPR), is presented to teams (not individuals) of federal employees who have made significant contributions in support of reinventing government principles. Those principles are: putting customers first, cutting red tape, empowering employees, and getting back to government basics. The award is the vice president's answer to yesterday's government and its $400 hammer. Fittingly, the award consists of a $6 hammer, a ribbon, and a note from Vice President Gore, all in an aluminum frame. About 600 Hammer Awards have been presented to teams composed of federal employees, state and local employees, and citizens who are working to build a better public sector. Vice President Gore is always looking to celebrate the accomplishments of teams demonstrating extraordinary effort toward implementing the goals of the NPR. Accordingly, there is no limited, annual window of opportunity for nominations imposed by the NPR. NPR encourages nominations throughout the year.
For further information contact:

National Performance Review
750 17th Street, NW, Suite 200
Washington, D.C. 20006
Phone: (202) 632-0150
Fax: (202) 632-0390
E-mail: http://www.npr.gov

The *National Association of Counties: Achievement Award Program* recognizes county governments that offer a new service to county residents in an effort to fill gaps in the availability of existing services, or that tap new revenue sources to improve the administration or enhance the cost-effectiveness of an existing county government program. County governments that upgrade the working conditions or level of training for county employees; enhance the level of citizen participation in, or the understanding of, government programs; provide information that facilitates effective public policy making; or promote intergovernmental cooperation and coordination in addressing shared problems are also recognized.

The *National Association of Counties: Disability Award* is sponsored by the National Association of Counties (NACo) in collaboration with the National Organization on Disabilities (NOD). It honors counties serving disabled Americans. This disability award program is just one of the ways NACo encourages members to further the goal of the full and active participation of people with disabilities in communities across the country. Through sponsorship by the J. C. Penney Co., the National Organization on Disability has provided NACo with funds to present a $1,000 cash award to a NACo member county with an outstanding program or project that enhances the ability of people with disabilities to participate in the processes, programs, and activities of county government.

The *National Association of Counties: Multicultural Diversity Award* is jointly sponsored by the National Association of Black County Officials (NABCO), the National Association of Hispanic County Officials (NAHCO), and Women Officials in NACo (WON). The award honors county governments for their efforts to promote cultural awareness and to recognize and appreciate the differences and similarities among people. Counties across the country have model diversity programs that recognize these differences. The Multicultural Diversity Award brings long overdue visibility to these programs, provides a showcase and reference from which other counties can benefit, and encourages continuing emphasis on this most important issue. This award is designed to recognize county governments for their effort to promote understanding of cultural differences within the community and the county workforce.

For further information contact:

National Association of Counties
440 First Street, NW
Washington, D.C. 20001

Phone: (202) 393-NACO
E-mail: http://www.naco.org

The *National Association of Towns and Townships* provides national recognition to outstanding small town leaders and their communities. For many years, the association presented the *Grassroots Government Leadership Award* to local officials from among the association's membership whose community service exhibited the highest standards of dedication, ability, creativity, and leadership.
 For further information contact:

National Association of Towns and Townships
444 North Capitol Street, Suite 294
Washington, D.C. 20001
Phone: (202) 624-3550
Fax: (202) 624-3554
E-mail: kjackson@sso.org

The *National Information Infrastructure (NII) Awards* recognize and honor superior accomplishment in applications of the Internet and the information highway. The awards program seeks out, celebrates, and showcases projects that show the world the power and potential of networked, interactive communications. The NII Awards Program is a learning community, and through demonstrating examples of excellence, NII hopes to facilitate the exchange of knowledge and experience, helping the public and private sectors make wiser and more effective use of communications technologies. Vice President Al Gore stated,

By offering these projects as examples of what is possible with the combination of technology and ingenuity, the NII Awards Program will inspire others and help us realize the potential of the information age. The program is a powerful way for information highway innovators to learn from each other.

The National Information Infrastructure Awards is a private-sector, non-partisan initiative.
 For further information contact:

info@gii-awards.com
staff@gii-awards.com

The *Public Service Excellence Award Program* is sponsored jointly at the federal, state, and local levels by the following:

Public Employees Roundtable
Office of Personnel Management
Federal Executive Boards/Federal Executive Associations
International City/County Management Association
National Governors' Association
National Association of Counties
National League of Cities
Conference of Mayors

Since 1985, Public Service Excellence Awards have paid tribute to programs that embody the highest standards of government in the nation. Awards go to federal, state, city, county, intergovernmental, and international government programs. In 1991, the Public Employees Roundtable (PER) expanded the program to include regional awards in several locations. Excellence Award winners represent public service at its best. The awards encourage innovation and excellence in government and reinforce pride in public service. The award program also calls public attention to the broad range of services provided by public employees and provides government at all levels the opportunity to showcase their outstanding programs. *Federal, State, City, County, International and Intergovernmental Awards Public Service Excellence Awards* recognize working units of two or more employees within federal, state, or local government agencies. The *Intergovernmental Award* recognizes the growing number of partnerships between units or levels of government. The *International Award* honors government programs that have an expressed mandate of international activity. The *Community Outreach Award* recognizes public employees who labor to improve their communities in ways outside of their jobs. Many retired public employees continue to serve their communities as well. The Community Outreach award, new in 1997, will honor a program or project that has a significant impact on the community and is performed either as a volunteer effort by current public employees, by a nonprofit group whose members are primarily public employees, or by a group of retired public employees.
   For further information contact:

Public Employees Roundtable
P.O. Box 14270

Washington, D.C. 20044-4270
Phone: (202) 927-5000
E-mail: http://adams.patriot.net/~permail/pseapp.htm

The *President's Quality Award Program,* sponsored by the Office of
Personnel Management, recognizes organizations for operational
performance excellence and improvement through two awards: the
Presidential Award for Quality and the *Quality Improvement Prototype
(QIP) Award.* Both are awarded to federal organizations on an annual
basis. Award recipients need to demonstrate results and improvement
on a wide range of indicators: customer related, operational, and
financial. Results reported need to address all stakeholders, customers, employees, suppliers, partners, special interest groups, Congress,
and the public. The award criteria address all aspects of high performance in an integrated and balanced way. This includes improvement of
the following: customer- and mission-related performance, productivity
in the use of all resources, speed and flexibility, product and service
quality, cost-effectiveness, and overall financial performance. The
criteria address key operating processes and results and are designed for diagnosis and feedback. All criteria directly relate to improving organization performance; nothing is included merely for
purposes of an award. The criteria do not call for specific practices or
organizational structures, because there are many possible approaches. The best choices depend upon many factors, including an
organization's type, size, strategy, and stage of development.
For further information contact:

U.S. Office of Personnel Management
1400 Wilson Boulevard, Room 702
Arlington, VA 22209
Phone: (703) 312-7335

The *RIT (Rochester Institute ofTechnology)/USA Today Quality Cup*
Competition (RIT/USA Today Quality Cup) honors teams that make
exceptional contributions to their employer's quality improvement
programs. The winning teams serve as national role models, encouraging others to adopt principles and practices that lead to continuous
improvement and customer satisfaction. The accomplishments of the
five winners of the 1996 Quality Cup were recounted in the May 3 issue
of *USA Today,* reaching 6 million readers. Awards are made in six
categories: educational institutions, government units and agencies,
health care organizations, manufacturing firms, service firms, and

small businesses. Both U.S. and foreign firms and organizations may nominate teams so long as the team members are employed in the United States. Multiple nominations are allowed.
For further information contact:

Carol Ann Skalski
USA Today
1000 Wilson Boulevard
Arlington, VA 22229
Phone: (703) 276-5890
E-mail: http://www.rit.edu/

Award programs are also sponsored by associations such as: American Public Works Association; Government Finance Officers Association; and International Personnel Management Association. Other programs and sponsors include Davis Productivity Awards, State of Florida; Energy Innovations Awards, Department of Energy; Historic Preservation Awards, Advisory Council on Historic Preservation; Innovative Financing Awards, Federal Highway Administration; Records Management Awards, International Institute of Municipal Clerks; Recycling Awards, Environmental Protection Administration; and Urban Land Institute Awards for Excellence.

Some of government's successes can be measured in the terminology of business: dollars saved, units of service delivered, rate of errors. But other successes—less tangible and just as important—are virtually unique to the public sector: national inspiration, individual optimism, level of literacy, sense of security, mastery of life skills, fostering of the arts. Public sector award programs recognize both dimensions of success, "bottom line" and "quality of life."

EVIDENCE OF SUCCESS

The Ford Foundation's Innovations in American Government Project at Harvard's Kennedy School, which is the most prominent and publicized of these recognition programs, has received well over 1,000 applications each year for nearly a decade. The program each year honors public initiatives that are exemplars of public sector innovation—because of both what they have accomplished and how they have accomplished it.

Harvard selects 25 semi-finalists, of which 10 receive major awards "on the basis of the creativity involved in the innovation, the significance of the problem it undertakes to solve, the program's value to the clients who benefit from it, and its transferability to other jurisdictions." Among its award recipients:

■ Massachusetts's Quincy District Court, which addresses the needs of women (more than one million nationally) who are beaten by husbands, lovers, or other men in their lives. Although police have begun taking domestic violence more seriously, other parts of the criminal justice system have not been as forthcoming. An exception is the Quincy Courts, serving the Norfolk County suburbs of Boston. The court encourages battered women to bring charges. To control abusers, the court confiscates weapons and enforces orders prohibiting alcohol and drug use. Offenders who continue to threaten violence are sentenced immediately. The most significant measure of the program's success is the decline in deaths from battering.

■ Virginia's Arlington County, which has developed Bilingual Outreach, a joint effort with private landlords and volunteers. Bilingual Outreach offers an array of free services and classes for new immigrants at six large apartment complexes in Arlington. Each center offers counseling programs ranging from how to use government services to advice on supermarket shopping and proper use of appliances. Programs to deal with the problems of teenagers are also available. Bilingual Outreach has served more than 12,000 immigrants since its inception a decade ago.

At Rutgers University, the National Center for Public Productivity's Exemplary State and Local Awards Program (EXSL) provides evidence of tangible accomplishments through productive public management: enhanced efficiency, capacity, and quality-of-life outcomes throughout the public sector. Since 1989, EXSL has selected 140 awardees through a peer review process in collaboration with the Section on Management Science and Policy Analysis of the American Society for Public Administration. Each award is the result of a rigorous selection process. Nominations are solicited widely and all of the nominees are well-documented, innovative programs. Each application is examined on a peer review basis and rated on multiple criteria by several judges from NCPP's panel of experts. Based on those objective ratings, semifinalists are selected for more intensive scrutiny. A committee is then convened to make the final selections.

Awards are made to projects and programs that produce significant cost savings, measurable increases in quality and productivity, and improvements in the effectiveness of government services. Programs chosen are highly rated on: program outputs, impact on quality of life of population served, cost-effectiveness, client support/satisfaction, innovative nature, obstacles or encumbrances that had to be overcome, nature of the problem that was addressed, degree of difficulty, and transferability or ability to serve as a model for other programs.

Significant improvements in the quality of services to the public have occurred when public employees have been empowered to undertake quality-improving, problem-solving initiatives. The creative, quality-oriented accomplishments that government's critics often call for are actually evident in virtually all parts of the public sector. EXSL programs address society's most difficult-to-solve problems, producing quality outcomes—especially improvement in clients' lives—such as: providing no-cost medical care for the indigent, unclogging court calendars, installing pollution and flood controls, expanding the supply of decent housing, increasing critical services to senior citizens, and rehabilitating youthful and older offenders.

EXSL award winners are evidence that producing public services is not only difficult work—but also anonymous work. Often only those at the very top are recognized. It is, however, just as important—if not more important—to recognize the people, the problem solvers, who make government work. Each award winner is represented today by a team of recipients, and EXSL recognizes both the organization's top policy-level official and the project team.

According to Governor Christine Whitman of New Jersey, speaking at an EXSL awards ceremony,

I could not help being impressed as I looked over the list of EXSL award winners. It is all too often that the public hears what is wrong in government; they do not hear what is right in government. When things are right, that good news should get out, and that is a part of what EXSL is about. Creativity and policy efforts should be rewarded. Award winners, who work for cities, counties and the state, took time to re-examine what they were doing, to see how they were doing it, and to take the risk, the risk of suggesting ways of doing it better. The wonderful thing is their efforts have paid off. They have helped children, veterans, the elderly, the environment and, from my perspective this is a wonderful outcome, they have helped the taxpayer. In fact a common theme among these award winners is that they all did more without asking for more.

I have noticed another common element in these uncommonly good programs. Many form innovative partnerships between the public and private sectors, and across agencies, departments, levels and even branches of the government, to show us what we can do when we start to think outside the normal bureaucratic box that controls our daily lives. All the honorees aimed for efficient delivery, for better outcomes for the people they serve. And they hit their mark in a variety of ways: improved technology, one-stop shopping, and integrated training and education. These people truly kept their eyes on tomorrow, and that is what government services should be all about. (Callahan, Holzer, & DeIorio, 1995, p. 36)

A brief overview of a few award-winning programs provides hard evidence that government is capable of, and in fact quite competent at, addressing multiple and diverse issues such as teenage pregnancies and farm safety. These award-winning programs also demonstrate that government routinely handles things that the average citizen rarely, consciously, thinks about.

CRIMINAL JUSTICE: ALTERNATIVES TO INCARCERATION

A significant portion of EXSL award-winning programs are recognized for their innovations in the field of criminal justice, particularly the very difficult goal of diverting likely youthful offenders away from an expensive and often counterproductive prison system.

Crisis Intervention. In Utah, timely intervention is the hallmark of the *Life Enhancement Alternative Program (L.E.A.P)*, a court-sanctioned project designed to provide early intervention to youths 14 years of age and younger with minor delinquent offenses. The intentions of the program are to provide immediate intervention and a comprehensive therapy milieu to help youths and their families deal with the crisis of delinquency; to help prevent youths from committing future crimes; and to help youths reach adulthood as healthy, happy, and productive citizens. L.E.A.P is offered free of charge and is part of the Salt Lake County Division of Youth Services. This 60-day program includes weekly law-related education classes, individual and family therapy, school tracking, and a community service project. The youth and his or her family earns points based on their active participation. Successful completion of L.E.A.P (achieving at least 500 points) may result in the case being closed with a nonjudicial standing by the Juvenile Court.

The *Community Intensive Supervision Project (CISP)* was developed and is operated by the Court of Common Pleas of Allegheny County, Pennsylvania, to provide a gamut of community-based treatment alternatives for chronic juvenile offenders. The CISP program operates intensive supervision programs for repeat offenders in neighborhoods in which the youth reside, allowing them to live at home under court supervision and avoiding additional institutional placements. Designed for male juvenile offenders aged 10 through 17, most youth admitted to the program are under court supervision at the time of their new offense and most youth enter CISP with property offenses or drug-related offenses. Intense supervision is provided to juvenile offenders, who report to specially designed neighborhood centers, 7 days a week from 4:00 p.m. to 10:00 p.m. Between 10:00 p.m. and 12:00 a.m., staff members return the youths to their homes and later return to knock on the door to make sure the youths are still home. Every youth in the program is electronically monitored, and these devices record all entries and exits from the youth's house by the youth. Drug testing is done on a random basis for every participant, and community service is required of all youthful offenders.

WATER: SAFEGUARDING QUALITY

Although the public sector usually produces services, its most tangible product may simply be water, the quality of which is basic to public health. We might take the quality of tap water for granted, but a reliable supply of high-quality (and safe) water results only when a very complex system of quality protection functions smoothly.

Assisting Local Governments. In response to the drastic decline of the commercial, recreational, and wildlife resources of the Chesapeake Bay, Virginia's government passed the Chesapeake Bay Preservation Act in 1988. Under the *Chesapeake Bay Local Assistance Program,* as mandated by this legislation, a citizens board, with state staff support, actively assists local governments to maximize the protection of the water quality of Chesapeake Bay, its tributaries, and other state waters. Legislative requirements are met through training, technology, grants, and consultation provided by the program. For example, the Chesapeake Bay Local Assistance Department (CBLAD) helps local governments meet state requirements to protect environmentally sensitive lands by incorporating water quality protection measures into zoning and subdivision ordinances. Technical assistance includes a state/local staff liaison network, a local assistance manual, computer software, training workshops, and an advisory review of project plans. Financial assistance provides grants for projects, computers and equipment, and personnel. CBLAD offers high-level technical expertise often out of reach of rural counties and small cities. Public participation also enables residents to address community goals and issues for the first time.

LIFE SKILLS:
INDEPENDENCE AND SAFETY

The ability of individuals to function productively in our society is often assumed. However, the public sector's clients—in housing or prisons, in schools or job programs—may have suffered setbacks or may have lost the ability to manage their lives. On the quality-of-life dimension of success, EXSL awardees have scored innovative successes in overcoming particularly challenging "people" problems.

Operation Fatherhood in New Jersey is designed to provide inner-city males between the ages of 13 and 19 with the skills and motivation to become successfully independent, healthy, and socially responsible young men. In 1989, Union Industrial Home for Children (UIH) and Planned Parenthood received a grant from the Robert Wood Johnson Foundation to begin solving the "other side" of the adolescent childbearing problem—the fathers. First Steps, UIH's first teen fathers program, was designed to provide young inner-city males with the skills and motivation necessary to become socially responsible young men. Building on the success of First Steps, UIH for Children was selected to participate in a pilot project designed to enhance the economic responsibility and family involvement of noncustodial fathers whose children are on welfare. The project is one of nine pilot sites, nationwide, selected to test the effectiveness of job training and supportive services for noncustodial fathers (between the ages of 16 and 45) whose children receive welfare.

Farming Safely in the Thumb is a program of the Huron County Health Department serving Huron, Sanilac, and Tuscola Counties in the state of Michigan. The program provides safety education and training to farmers and farm workers, including family members, who are confronted by the problems inherent in a rapidly changing agricultural environment of new pesticides and equipment, as well as the continued usage of old and possibly dangerous farming equipment. These conditions require preventive measures to reduce farming-related injuries and deaths. Farming Safely in the Thumb is a multifaceted safety education and prevention program developed for farm workers. The overall goal of the program is the reduction of agriculture-related injuries and deaths. Farming Safely helps in the identification of hazards and provides recommendations for eliminating them or at least increasing skills for dealing with those that cannot be eliminated. Farm Bureau and 4-H courses, such as "Tractor and Farm Machinery Safety" for youth 10 years and older, provide safety education and a Certificate of Training. The county also conducts First-on-the-Scene Workshops that provide training on "what to do before EMS arrives" in the event of a traumatic injury.

PRODUCING PUBLIC SERVICES

Successful problem-solving projects—award winning or routine—are not the "commonsense" solutions typically posed by politicians, voters, corporate critics, and the media: "cut the fat" or "cut back management," "economize" or "privatize," "work harder" or "work smarter," "businesslike management" or "Japanese management." If only such straightforward adages described what public organizations needed, then government's efficiency would not be at issue.

But simple prescriptions are not very useful. They are based upon popular misperceptions of public management. They are contrary to the complex problem-solving processes governments (or private organizations of comparable size) require in order to address our society's most difficult to solve problems, such as crime, pollution, and homelessness. Rather, the

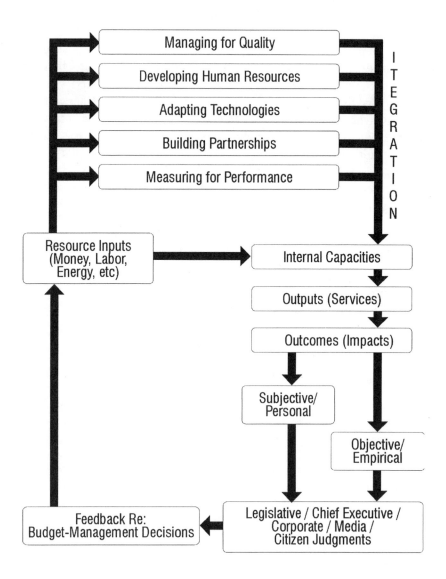

Figure 1.1. Comprehensive Public Sector Productivity Improvement

provision and improvement of services, in government *or* in the most profitable private sector firms, is complex and requires hard, detailed work. As a function of this organizational and analytical momentum, today, to produce public services, the best public organizations have developed multiple, reinforcing capacities. Award-winning government agencies typically (a) apply quality management principles, (b) use measurement as a decision-making tool, (c) invest in human resource development and organizational learning, (d) adapt new technologies, and (e) develop partnerships—with the private sector, with other governmental and nonprofit agencies, and between management and labor. We have found those approaches to be consistently apparent in award-winning cases, as illustrated in Figure 1.1, Public Sector Productivity Improvement: A Multifaceted Approach.

In the following chapters, EXSL cases are classified according to an emphasis on one of these five primary approaches to public sector productivity improvement. Although each EXSL case has been categorized by its primary orientation to one of these five emphases, many are crosscutting, incorporating several productivity improvement practices. The cases we have chosen are examples of the state of the art and are only a sampling of productive innovations.

Each emphasis improves the utilization of resources (e.g., tax dollars, labor, energy, capital) in order to organize internal capacities more efficiently and effectively, which produces outputs (i.e., services) leading to expected outcomes (i.e., the impacts of those services).

Within the context of Figure 1.1, *productivity* is the ratio of outputs and outcomes (work done, products distributed, services rendered, impact achieved) to inputs. Productivity *improvement* has to do with favorable changes in that ratio. Expectations of productivity improvement in the public sector must be tempered by recognition that there are differences between various ratios (or definitions) of improvement, and that several of the five possibilities below represent difficult circumstances that any organization—private or public—would be hard-pressed to meet (see also Figure 1.2). In each of the five emphases below, award-winning government has successfully responded to challenges the private sector would have considered impossible or unprofitable to confront.

1. *Doing the Same With Less.* Resource inputs decline, but outputs/ outcomes are expected to remain constant. This represents a cutback

HOW IS PRODUCTIVITY IMPROVED?

1. SAME OUTPUT/OUTCOMES

LESS INPUT

2. MORE OUTPUT/OUTCOMES

SAME INPUT

3. MUCH MORE OUTPUT/OUTCOMES

MUCH LESS INPUT

4. MUCH MORE OUTPUT/OUTCOMES

MORE INPUT

5. LESS OUTPUT

MUCH LESS INPUT

Figure 1.2. How Is Productivity Improved?

management situation in which management is forced to respond productively when confronted with budget cutbacks in real dollars. For example,
faced with a cutback in staff, a state mental health facility may reorganize,
allowing for the same level of services with more efficient use of remaining
staff.

2. *Doing More With the Same Resources.* Although resource inputs remain
constant, public servants may be asked to improve outputs/outcomes.
Many critics of government, particularly elected officials, argue this case.
They often expect "quick fixes" based on limited perspectives or critiques
by groups external to the agency. For example, they might propose that
each social services worker increase applications processed by 25%. This
might be a reasonable goal, but cannot be implemented instantly, only as
better management of inputs improves outputs.

3. *Doing Much More With Much Less.* In the most difficult case, resource inputs may decline substantially, but government is pressured to improve outputs/outcomes substantially. Some elected officials and private sector critics advocate this scenario. It is, however, almost always based upon unreasonable and naive assumptions; for instance, that waste is of enormous proportions. Without the ability to invest in improved capacities while maintaining adequate services to all applicants, this case is less reasonable than doing more with the same resources.

4. *Doing Much More With a Little More.* If some resource inputs can be increased moderately, then outputs/outcomes may improve substantially. This is a more likely case, as it allows for continued modest investments in improved productive capacity. But in the short run, a true productivity program is more likely to experience temporarily decreasing productivity—constant outputs while inputs increase modestly to allow for improved internal capacities, which will then increase outputs at a later stage. For example, in a state correctional facility, investments in training, buildings, and equipment may be necessary in Year 1 prior to improved correctional services in Year 2.

5. *Doing Somewhat Less With Much Less.* If some inputs decline substantially, then public managers are challenged to limit the decline in outputs/outcomes. Although the output to input ratio is apparently increasing, drastic cutbacks in resources often result in cutbacks in services, which fall most heavily on those citizens least likely to have alternatives. In a situation of deep cutbacks a municipal college, for example, may be forced to cut psychological counseling services to students—most of whom are unlikely to be able to purchase such services privately.

CONCLUSION

Government does solve problems. The cases highlighted in this chapter provide ample evidence of that. From preserving natural resources to ensuring the safety of farmers, from providing short-term housing for the homeless to instilling responsibility in teenage fathers, the problems addressed by government are multiple and complex. Moreover, virtually all state and local governments are confronting existing and emerging problems with far fewer resources than just a decade ago.

Good things are happening in the public sector. Creative solutions to pressing problems are implemented on a daily basis. We do not, however, hear enough about the positive accomplishments. The failures of government are what dominate the airwaves, the headlines, and the water cooler conversations. We would prefer to see a middle ground established where both the good and the bad aspects of government are honestly portrayed and openly discussed. Constructive dialogue and positive examples can provide opportunities for bad programs to become good and for good programs to become great.

If citizens hear only about the failures and inefficiencies of the public sector, they will believe that government is incapable of doing anything right. Citizens will expect less, and public servants may actually end up giving less, when the dominant perception is "it can't be done." A self-fulfilling prophecy emerges, and society eventually gets what it expects and possibly what it deserves. If as citizens we believe that government is unresponsive, that is most likely what we will get—unresponsive government. However, if we believe that government is responsive, or at least has the potential to be responsive, and we work with and support our public servants, then we are more likely to get better government. If as citizens we become involved in the process of government in a proactive manner, our expectations, as well as the performance of the public sector, will markedly increase.

The people who work in government are dedicated to the public service and dedicated to improving the quality of life of their fellow citizens in spite of seemingly insurmountable odds. They deserve to be commended for their efforts rather than criticized and condemned. As we argued above, people who work in government are different than people who work in the private sector. Intrinsic rewards, such as recognition, and acknowledgment that they are "doing the right thing," are far greater motivators than money and a corner office with a view. We should, therefore, consciously try to acknowledge and reward the accomplishments of these individuals. The criticism they suffer on a daily basis, even from the clients they serve, only serves to undermine their ability to perform and function effectively.

Successes are routine, yet they are taken for granted and rarely acknowledged. We expect our mail to be delivered on time and our garbage to be collected on a regular basis. The school bus should arrive promptly at 7:35 so we can leave for work on time, and of course the public highways have to be in good repair and the public transportation systems have to be operating on schedule so we actually get to the office on time. It is when these systems and services do not work that we become vocal complainants. For the most part, when they do work, we remain silent. Public servants must become advocates, or champions, of the public sector. They need to stand up to the critics of government and continually support and promote the efforts of the public sector. The examples we highlight in this book and, by extension, in a wide array of award programs, can provide a solid foundation for arguments defending the public service and the public sector.

REFERENCES

Ammons, D. N. (1991). Reputational leaders in local government productivity and innovation. *Public Productivity and Management Review, 15*(1), 19-43.

American Society for Public Administration. (1992-1996). *National and chapter awards programs*. Washington, DC: Author.

Brooks, S. (1987). *Who's in charge: The mixed ownership corporation in Canada*. Ottawa: Institute for Research on Public Policy.

Cacioppe, R., & Mock, P. (1984). A comparison of the quality of work experience in government and private organizations. *Human Relations, 37*(11), 923-940.

Callahan, K., Holzer, M., & DeIorio, J. (Eds.). (1995). *Reinventing New Jersey*. Burke, VA: Chatelaine.

Carr, C. (1991). Los Angeles County Productivity Managers Network: An alternative to traditional productivity program management. *Public Productivity and Management Review, 15*(1), 47-59.

Dobbs, M. F. (1992). *Los Angeles County productivity study*. Unpublished manuscript, Department of Public Administration, San Diego State University.

Downs, T. (1988, March). Reflections of a public service junkie. *PM*, pp. 7-8.

Frederickson, H. G., & Hart, D. K. (1985). The public service and the patriotism of benevolence. *Public Administration Review, 45*, 547-553.

Local Government Information Network (LOGIN). (n.d.). [Computer program]. St. Paul, MN: William C. Norris Institute.

Moe, R., & Gilmour, R. S. (1995). Rediscovering the principles of public administration. *Public Administration Review, 55*, 135-146.

Nalbandian, J., & Edwards, J. T. (1983). The values of public administrators: A comparison with lawyers, social workers and business administrators. *Review of Public Personnel Administrators, 4*, 114-127.

National Academy of Public Administration. (1990). *Awards description*. Washington, DC: Author.

Osborne, D., & Gaebler, T. (1992). *Reinventing government*. Reading, MA: Addison-Wesley.

Poister, T. H. (1988). Success stories in revitalizing public agencies. *Public Productivity Review, 11*(3), 27-28.

Public Employees Roundtable. (n.d.). *Unsung heroes* [Brochure]. Washington, DC: Author.

Public Employees Roundtable. (1987-1996). *Unsung heroes* [Newsletter]. Washington, DC: Author.

Rainey, H. G. (1982). Reward preferences among public and private managers: In search of the service ethic. *American Review of Public Administration, 16,* 440-448.

Rainey, H. G. (1991). *Understanding and managing public organizations.* San Francisco: Jossey-Bass.

Rainey, H. G., Backoff, R. W., & Levine, C. N. (1976). Comparing public and private organizations. *Public Administration Review, 36,* 233-244.

Reeves, R. (1989, August/September). Careers in the public service. *Crisis, 96,* 22.

Rosenbloom, D. H. (1993). *Public administration: Understanding management, politics, and law in the public sector.* New York: McGraw-Hill.

Rosenbloom, D. H., & Carroll, J. D. (1990). *Toward constitutional competence: A casebook for public administrators.* Englewood Cliffs, NJ: Prentice Hall.

Siedman, E. (1984, Summer). Of games and gains . . . *The Bureaucrat,* pp. 4-8.

Six bright stars: Another lustrous year in the public service. (1990). In *Public papers of The Fund for the City of New York.* New York: Fund for the City of New York.

Smetanka, M. J. (1990, October 28). Mid-career professionals are turning to teaching. *Minneapolis Star-Tribune,* p. 1.

Streib, G., & Waugh, W. L., Jr. (1991). Administrative capacity and the barriers to effective county management. *Public Productivity and Management Review, 15*(1), 61-70.

Wilson, W. (1887). The study of administration. *Political Science Quarterly, 2,* 197-222.

Wittmer, D. (1991). Serving the people or serving for pay. *Public Productivity and Management Review, 14,* 355-367.

2

MANAGEMENT
FOR QUALITY

> **Managing for Quality**
>
> Top Management Support ─
> Customer Focus ─
> Long-Term Strategic Planning ─
> Employee Training and Recognition ─
> Employee Empowerment and Teamwork ─
> Measurement and Analysis ─
> Quality Assurance ─

GOVERNMENT'S MISSIONS ARE COMPLEX

In the continuous search for improved methods, the public service is more than willing to consider, and then often borrow and adapt, concepts that have become popular among their private counterparts. For instance, "quality" has been a corporate buzzword, and the quality movement in government draws heavily on decades of industrial quality improvement work in the private sector, such as that of Deming (1986) and Juran (1988). Adapting business-oriented definitions, Cohen and Brand (1993) suggest a definition of Total Quality Management (TQM) for the public sector:

- *Total* implies applying the search for quality to every aspect of work, from identifying customer needs to aggressively evaluating whether the customer is satisfied.
- *Quality* means meeting and exceeding customer expectations.
- *Management* means developing and maintaining the organizational capacity to constantly improve quality. (p. xi)

According to the authors,

> the same principles of total quality management used in private industry are creating a quiet revolution in the public sector. . . . To improve quality of service, increase productivity, and reduce waste, more and more government managers—from Little Rock to Washington—are turning to TQM. (Cohen & Brand, 1993, p. xii)

The U.S. General Accounting Office (GAO; 1991) surveyed high-scoring Baldridge Award applicants (the Baldridge Award is a national competition, administered by the Department of Commerce, primarily for the private sector) and concluded that six features were important:

1. Corporate attention is focused on meeting customer quality requirements.
2. Management leads the way in disseminating TQM values throughout the organization.
3. Employees are asked and empowered to improve all key business processes continuously.
4. Management nurtures a flexible and responsive corporate culture.
5. Management systems support fact-based decision making.
6. Partnerships with suppliers improve product or service delivery.

But industrially based quality management cannot simply be transplanted to the public sector. According to the Federal Quality Institute (FQI; Mizaur, 1993), government's task is more complex: "Private sector customer agendas are often straightforward . . . even with multiple customers . . . there is usually substantial congruence on the primary agenda. However, in many Government agencies customer agendas may be varied, complex, or competing" (p. 371).[1]

In contrast to narrower private sector definitions, FQI's own definition (Mizaur, 1993) gives equal weight to the stakes of employees and funders:

Quality management is a strategic integrated management system for achieving customer satisfaction through the involvement of all employees and continuous improvement of all the organization's processes and use of resources. All three stakehold agendas—that of customer, employee, funder—must be served equally. (U.S. FQI, pp. 371-377)

Consistent with the comprehensive FQI definition, Hyde (1992; U.S. FQI, 1990) sets forth seven key factors for successful implementation of quality improvement programs based primarily on the FQI model, including elements of private sector TQM approaches that he viewed as relevant to government. In order for the public sector to implement quality management initiatives successfully, public organizations must have the following:

1. top management support
2. customer focus
3. long-term strategic planning
4. employee training and recognition
5. employee empowerment and teamwork
6. measurement and analysis of products and processes
7. quality assurance

Each of Hyde's seven factors is confirmed in practice by EXSL awardees who are committed to a basic TQM principle: continuous improvement. They work with the workforce to identify opportunities for improvement, and then implement related solutions. These seven factors serve as the framework for presenting the cases in this chapter.

TOP MANAGEMENT SUPPORT

The commitment of top management is a necessary first step in disseminating quality improvement values throughout the organization. Leaders must be committed to achieving excellence. That commitment is neither just a "signal"; nor is it superficial "lip service." Quality-oriented changes will result only from basic reorientations of an organization's culture, and change of that magnitude must start with changes in behavior at the top as a model throughout the hierarchy. Leaders must be willing to relinquish some of their control and become facilitators for change (Hunt, 1993). Quality-oriented leaders in the public sector are also

committed to the creation of an ethical climate in terms of the dissemi-
nation of quality improvement values throughout the organization.

Beyond Expectations. Discouraged by the lack of an increase in productivity after incorporating traditional MBO techniques, top management in
the city of Dayton, Ohio decided to implement a distinctly different
approach, *Management by Unreasonable Objectives.*
    Under the traditional MBO philosophy, the manager tries to establish
organizational objectives that are clear and understandable, verifiable,
results oriented, and properly written. Once the department or division
attains the original objectives, it is the manager's responsibility to encourage annual, incremental improvements.
    Management by Unreasonable Objectives (MBUO), as incorporated
in Dayton, departs from the traditional MBO philosophy on the last
point. According to the philosophy of MBUO, an organization needs a
consistently good set of objectives merely to maintain an efficient operation. In order to change and bring about quality improvements, however,
an organization needs to set unreasonable objectives. The MBUO philosophy assumes that the only reasonable way a manager can make
dramatic changes is to establish unreasonable objectives. It incorporates
the best of the traditional MBO techniques with a quality most managers
possess in abundance: unreasonableness.

    Managers in Dayton's Department of Finance set unreasonable objec-
tives to bring about radical change: to enable managers and employees
to "think outside the box" and overcome that dreaded "But we've always
done it that way" syndrome.
    The three basic tenets of MBUO are

1. there must be a clearly stated objective that can be measured and verified;
2. the objective has to be so good that the workers and the managers emphati-
   cally agree that it is a worthwhile goal; and
3. the objective must be so unreasonable that the workers' and managers' first
   response is that it cannot be done. Any sense of an incremental objective
   must be dismissed.

MBUO promotes innovation and encourages employees to think creatively and take risks. To reach unreasonable objectives, managers must
break through the typical restraints of the mind. Hard results of these

initiatives are substantial productivity, growth, increased revenues, improved quality, and an efficient and proud staff. In order for this approach to work, managers have to be champions of the cause and encourage what may be considered "unorthodox" behavior to achieve quality outcomes. The bottom line is that MBO techniques make people work harder; MBUO techniques make people work smarter.

Revitalized Enforcement. In Phoenix, Arizona, the child support collection system had grown over the years in fits and starts. The system reflected many years of "patched together" processes that were designed to address specific problems or new requirements that arose, instead of improving the overall system. The system became a monolith of outmoded procedures, and the only way to correct the problem was through a complete overhaul.

By applying Total Quality Management principles to government, the *Process Improvement Initiative* revitalized the Division of Child Support Enforcement (DCSE). Innovative approaches to problem solving focused on replacing outdated, ineffective processes, resulting in dramatic improvements. Rather than concentrate on restructuring the organization, employees focused on revitalizing processes. Employees were responsible for identifying problems as well as designing and implementing solutions. Working with the full support of management, the employees incorporated new procedures that increased the number of child support orders established and enforced, decreased the time it takes to establish and collect on a child support order, and provided improved customer service.

A complete review of the Division's procedures enabled employees to identify problem areas. By removing scores of unnecessary steps and streamlining hundreds more, the Process Improvement Initiative Team was able to recommend 19 projects to streamline and to reduce the cycle time (the time it takes to work a case through establishment and collection of a child support order) by 74%. Under the outmoded process, custodial parents waited 187 business days, more than 8 months, to start receiving child support. Under the new process, a child support order can be established or enforced in less than 48 business days.

CUSTOMER FOCUS

Public sector organizations often have a captive clientele. Traditionally, many agencies (and service providers) take the individuals they interact with for granted—students in a classroom, welfare recipients in a waiting room—rather than viewing them as clients with particular needs. Forward-looking public organizations, however, have adopted a different model, citizen-as-customer, through which they consciously identify obstacles to improved client services and then work to solve those problems. They respect and respond to customers. As Hunt (1993) argues, successful organizations engage in open, continuous, two-way communication with their customers and utilize ongoing measures of customer satisfaction to alter and improve their services and processes.

Avoiding Costly Problems. Customer quality requirements have been defined as enhanced "Quality of Life," by the *Tenant Assistance Program* (TAP) of the Massachusetts Housing Finance Agency. The overall goal of the program is to assist tenants and enhance their ability to function as productive citizens and cooperative neighbors. In doing this, the quality of life for all residents of public housing is vastly improved, which in turn preserves affordable housing opportunities within the state.

The TAP program trains thousands of property management staff in prevention and intervention techniques in an effort to avoid confrontation with tenants. This training, coupled with tenant education and crisis intervention services, fosters a positive, proactive relationship between tenants and management. In fact, TAP was recognized as the first concerted effort on the part of a public housing agency in this country to address the alcohol and drug abuse problems of their tenants. In public housing, the real costs of alcohol and drug abuse are counted not only in terms of the devastated lives of users, but also in terms of property damage due to fires and floods, unpaid rents, legal costs, high insurance premiums, and the resulting difficulty in preserving affordable housing.

One of the most notable aspects of the TAP program is the cooperation of every member of the property management staff—from the managers, to the receptionists, to the maintenance workers. Everyone on the housing management staff participates in training that addresses the situations they face on a daily basis, including the identification of substance abuse, effective crisis intervention skills, codependency, cultural diversity, AIDS, attitudes and prejudices, and conflict resolution techniques. Through this comprehensive and inclusive training effort, the property management staff has worked effectively with tenants to resolve issues before they escalate into full-blown problems. Since TAP's inception, property management staff members are able to identify substance abusers and work with them to make sure they get appropriate treatment rather than eviction.

TAP's Tenant Education Programs, including the formation of resident associations, are available at every public housing property in the state. The resident associations are intended to bring residents together and to foster a sense of community in the housing complex. Some of the programs provided through the resident associations include an arts and crafts program for children, parenting classes for new and expecting parents, affordable healthy-cooking classes, and regular exercise classes. Participation in the various Tenant Education Programs has led to a greater sense of community among the residents and to new friendships. Prior to the Tenant Education Programs, residents in Massachusetts public housing had the tendency to keep to themselves and many felt that all they had in common with their neighbors was their address.

Not only has TAP literally saved lives and made public housing a nicer place to live, but it has also preserved affordable housing and enhanced the quality of life for all the residents living in public housing. It has reduced management costs due to fewer vacancies and abandoned apartments, far fewer fires, and less property damage. The changes in management style increased the stability and standard of living and resulted in nearly $1 million in insurance premium discounts.

LONG-TERM STRATEGIC PLANNING

Government must often react to changes in its environment—an increased budget cut, a decreased tax base, an unfunded mandate, a change in elected officials. Those are all environmental constants, and adept public managers have developed excellent coping skills for maintaining their balance. But the most effective top officials have also undertaken deliberate planning to anticipate and then steer change in a productive, quality-enhancing direction.

Competitive Bidding. Indianapolis recognized that the marketplace in which cities operate has changed. Major cities no longer compete against each other for businesses and families. They compete against their suburbs, and they are losing. Suburbs generally offer lower taxes, less crime, better schools, and fewer environmental risks to businesses. Large numbers of businesses and families are migrating to the suburbs, leaving the financially disadvantaged behind. Indianapolis's effort to alleviate some of these structural disincentives—to decrease migration to the suburbs—largely rests on the provision of some city services through competitive bidding. *Competition and Costing* is a program designed to make the public sector more competitive. Service delivery is improved through competition, rather than privatization. Instead of limiting itself to the option of turning a city service over to a private vendor, city employees are encouraged to bid in competition with the private sector. What makes competition possible is activity-based costing, a financial and accounting tool that determines the internal costs of government activities that city employees can use in their bids. Competition improves the delivery of services by inducing private sector vendors and city workers to be far more efficient and creative about how to provide improved services at lower costs.

By enabling city workers to compete fairly against private sector vendors, Indianapolis has reduced its budget by $10 million. The savings are reinvested in the city, allowing Indianapolis to put more police officers on the streets and to invest in a $500 million infrastructure rebuilding program, the largest in city history, without raising taxes. The program emphasizes competition, innovation, and entrepreneurial thought among city employees, together with the adaptation of activity-based costing to the public sector.

Structured Planning. In the City of Fremont, California, management nurtures a flexible and responsive organizational culture as part of a structured strategic planning process. The *Strategic Planning for Unified Decision Support* (SPUDS), is an innovative approach that involves employees at all levels and requires that every government department, with substantial input from employees within their respective departments as well as employees from other departments, develop a strategic plan. Reaching out to other departments in the planning stage made employees realize how interconnected they are and enabled them to discuss ways in which they could assist each other in providing comprehensive services to the community. As a result, each strategic plan is a response to the need for long-term vision and the development of interdepartmental cooperation to implement that vision.

Strategic planning is now a critical part of the city's operations. A new "breed" of public organizational management, it both values the accumulated wisdom of city staff professionals and demands that a context be established for budget requests. SPUDS offers the rare opportunity for staff to take a step back from everyday affairs and crises in order to evaluate the environment, to anticipate, to plan, and ultimately to gain control of a project.

Each year, every city department enters into strategic planning sessions led by facilitators from the Management Analysis Division. In these sessions, city staff define the department's overall mission, review the past year to identify key issues facing the department, develop strategies and action plans to respond to those issues, and finally identify other city departments to cooperate with in order to achieve interdepartmental cooperation, which is critical to the department's strategic plan. The SPUDS process coincides with the preparation of the annual budget document in order to create an interactive relationship between financial decision making and organizational planning; it provides a strategic context for budget decisions and establishes a financial context for operational planning.

SPUDS has produced many concrete results. The Public Works Department identified the need to standardize their definitions of service levels, and created new service definitions and an action plan to ensure the new standards are met. The Fire Department administration recognized its need to become an integral and professional contributor to the central administration of the city, and restructured its organization to respond more effectively to the community's needs (not the least of which is the creation and management of three new fire stations). A cooperative effort between the Human Services Youth and Family Counseling Center and the Police Department produced a unique and multi-faceted program to respond to substance abuse problems. The Finance Department, in order to provide more responsive and useful service to departments, implemented a philosophy of decentralization by first developing finance staff teams dedicated to specific departments, and then by placing emphasis on building greater financial expertise capacity within each department.

A critical part of SPUDS was a participant survey, which was sent to all those involved after the annual process was completed. The first year's participant response was overwhelmingly favorable: 88.7% of the respondents felt the process significantly helped them think about their departments' goals.

EMPLOYEE TRAINING AND RECOGNITION

The highest quality goals of the most well-intended public sector leaders will remain unfulfilled if organizations are not prepared to produce, and the prerequisite for any productivity-quality effort is the preparation of the most important, most expensive organizational elements—its human resources. If employees are to produce at higher levels of quality, then the training that is prerequisite to service delivery must also be delivered at high levels. Although training is one of the first targets of policy-and management-level budget cutters, exemplary programs do not sacrifice that capacity-building investment for short-term savings. Quality-improving organizations must continuously improve workforce skills.

Caring for Children. In North Carolina, the *T.E.A.C.H. Early Childhood Project* addresses the need for qualified and trained personnel to work in child care centers throughout the state. More than 158,000 children spend their days in one of North Carolina's 3,400 licensed child care centers or 3,300 registered family day care homes. Before the project started, these children were being cared for by child care staff that typically had no formal education past high school, made less than $5.25 per hour, and left the field at a rate of 38% per year.

T.E.A.C.H. is based on the principle of partnership and brings together the statewide community college system, child care staff, employing agencies, and an extensive scholarship program. The Project's goal is to affect positively the quality of care that children who are cared for in child care centers throughout North Carolina receive by addressing some of the issues that have resulted in a statewide, and indeed national, child care staffing crisis.

T.E.A.C.H. provides educational scholarship opportunities for child care staff to attend college to further their education in early childhood. These programs are designed to be inclusive of different educational levels upon entry and are structured to offer a variety of options that meet the needs of the diversity of child care settings in the state.

Higher education has been linked to more positive caregiver behavior, a greater likelihood of providing developmentally appropriate activities, and to the following positive outcomes for children: better language skills, lower levels of apathy, increased cooperative behavior, and greater task persistence. Conversely, high turnover rates have been linked to negative outcomes for children: lower developmental levels in play with peers, lower perceptions of own competence, evidence of greater insecurity, and poorer academic performance at the end of first grade. Research has demonstrated that among the characteristics that contribute to the quality of an early childhood setting are higher caregiver education level and low staff turnover. T.E.A.C.H. improves the delivery of child care services by providing child care staff with affordable educational opportunities.

EMPLOYEE EMPOWERMENT AND TEAMWORK

Producing quality is almost never the effort of only one individual. High-quality services are produced by teams, and those teams are empowered to solve problems. Teams recognize the reality of interdependence: Individual service providers function only within a support system of many colleagues who are often invisible to the service recipient. Hospital medical personnel are dependent not only on each other (doctors, nurses, technicians) but on intake, maintenance, billing, and food staff, as well as volunteers. Teachers are similarly dependent on personnel in transportation, maintenance, pupil personnel services, and administration. And problems of quality in a hospital, school, or any other public organization are best solved by those closest to the problem, including staff in both line (direct providers) and support (indirect providers) roles.

Involving Employees. Effective quality leadership must lead to employee participation in problem solving, and in Pinellas County, Florida, employees are asked and empowered to improve continuously all key "business" processes. In 1988, Pinellas County established a comprehensive *"Quality Improvement Program"* to facilitate greater employee involvement and improved municipal services to county residents. The objective is to increase employee productivity with an emphasis on quality and efficiency. The program encourages greater employee involvement as the means to more efficient, higher-quality services to county residents.

The Pinellas County's Board of Commissioners developed a plan based on employee involvement. Its seven-member Quality Planning Council established a set of standards and goals for the efficient operation of the county government. Employee participation is the cornerstone of this effort, which rewards increased involvement and achievements with monetary incentives as well as gifts, paid leave, and public recognition. Employees have been awarded for their efforts in loss and prevention, in damage control, for their expressed commitment to the community, and for leadership initiatives. Employees are honored at various banquets, luncheons, dinners, and other events that foster a greater sense of involvement and participation. Peer recognition goes a long way as it acknowledges the accomplishments of individuals who strive to improve the quality of services they provide and encourages others to do the same.

Annual financial savings, as a result of the quality initiatives, topped $650,000 dollars in the first year. The savings were realized through the more efficient use of resources, time management, and employee-generated innovations. The program also stresses specific quality objectives including preserving and protecting the environment and water resources, encouraging greater participation in recycling efforts, and improving public safety.

The concept of employee empowerment and participation drive this quality improvement program, as evidenced by increased team building and the flow of innovative ideas emanating from county employees. The costs associated with running the Pinellas County Quality Improvement Program are minimal, approximately $20,000 annually for printing, incentives, awards, and ceremonies. Sound, productive management also occurs outside the "total quality" umbrella and includes a wide range of techniques such as restructuring, organizational development, strategic planning, facility planning, and performance standards.

■ MEASUREMENT AND ANALYSIS OF PRODUCTS AND PROCESSES

Quality-enhancing public sector programs value feedback. They establish a data collection system, continually measure their internal and external outputs/outcomes, analyze those measures for indications of problems, and then approach those problems as opportunities for improving service delivery.

Analyzing Ambulance Operations. An important element of management for quality is that management systems be structured to support fact-based decision making. Such decisions were the outcome of the District of Columbia's major operations improvement initiative involving the Emergency Medical Services (EMS) system. The study, "Improving Ambulance Operation: A Blueprint for Change," was conducted by the District's internal management consulting arm, Productivity Management Services, and it examined the critical functions of the EMS system, which serves over 620,000 area residents.

Inadequate emergency care, as perceived by D.C. residents and the staff of area hospitals, prompted the study. Residents complained of poor response times, human errors in dispatching calls, and allegations that ambulance crews were getting lost trying to locate addresses. The study, which was extensive and required more than 10,000 staff hours, examined almost every aspect of the EMS, including the organizational structure, existing channels of communication, size and number of response units, fleet configuration, EMS training, and various other operational and personnel-oriented issues. The study recommended upgrading the efficiency and reliability of the existing emergency medical fleet, including the reassignment of key EMS personnel. This project also focused on the changing role of emergency ambulance service from that of simply "getting the patient to the hospital" to today's sophisticated mobile intensive care units.

The project resulted in increased ambulance availability, decreased response time, more balanced workloads, and a reduction in dispatch time. Specifically, program changes that were made as a result of OCA's analyses were: (a) Peak load work schedules were instituted, replacing static work schedules; (b) changes were implemented in ambulance unit locations; (c) a no-cost proposal to improve response time and unit availability was developed by eliminating two deployment policies that adversely affected system performance; (d) a long-range implementation plan was developed for upgrading the fleet to an all Advanced Life Support (ALS) system; and (e) determinations were made as to how many ambulances were needed by time of day and location to meet response time targets under different operating scenarios.

The program has achieved the following results: (a) the probability that no unit would be available during peak hours dropped from 22% to less than 1%; (b) the number of times no unit was available in each 24-hour period dropped by 55% (from 20 occurrences per day to 9); (c) response time across regions of the city was more balanced. The gap between the best- and worst-served areas of the city was reduced by 57%

(from a 90-second gap down to a 39-second gap); and (d) workloads across ambulance units were more balanced. The average workload per unit dropped by 20% (from 29 to 23). In addition, (e) ambulance utilization rates during peak hours, which at 75% were twice as high as the recommended level of 35% to 40%, dropped to 61%; (f) a 22% reduction in time from call to dispatch occurred as a result of changes implemented in the communications division; and (g) response time dropped by 30 seconds during a 2-month shake-down test.

QUALITY ASSURANCE

Measurement and analysis is useful as a relative approach, that is, as a process of benchmarking against past performance in pursuit of continual improvement. But a capacity for measurement and analysis is also important against an objective, external benchmark such as a professional standard or the performance standards of other, similar organizations. Assuring quality means assuring that those standards are met.

Acting, Not Reacting. The Emergency Medical Service of Lee County, Florida's *Medical Quality Assurance Program* is an ongoing comprehensive medical quality assurance program designed to achieve and maintain an optimal level of pre-hospital patient care for the residents of the county. It addresses the inability to measure appropriately the quality and level of pre-hospital patient care provided by the county's emergency medical service. Prior to the implementation of this quality assurance program, problems of improper patient care were dealt with in a reactionary nature.

The intent of this program is to replace reactive responses with proactive approaches to health care that will result in a preventive orientation on the part of both the patient and the provider. Components of this program include direct review of reports of each ambulance "run" and in-field observation, as well as the evaluation of medications, medical equipment, protocols, and procedures. For example, during the analysis of certain medical equipment it was found that their use was ineffective in certain cases. By narrowing the inclusion criteria regarding the employment of this equipment, a significant reduction in expenditures was achieved.

As part of this quality assurance program, a follow-up reporting system was established with the local medical facilities. This opened a channel of communication with the medical professionals at those facilities that had, until then, remained unused. As a result of this enhanced communication, Lee County Emergency Medical Service was able to measure the true caliber of care given to patients.

Through the intensive scrutiny of run reports, Lee County EMS was able to identify undesirable trends in patient care and inform their personnel of such problems. Once personnel were informed of a deficiency, the appropriate remedial actions could take place. This heightened awareness, coupled with a positive work environment, decreased the likelihood of costly medical malpractice litigation.

CONCLUSION

Although neither *TQM* nor *quality improvement* were terms generally found in the public sector literature as late as 1988, the past decade has witnessed accelerated momentum under this improvement rubric. But quality improvement in government, particularly state and local government, is not merely a recent phenomenon. Comprehensive productivity-quality improvements have long been characteristic of government in an environment of increasing demands and reduced resources (Poister, 1992, p. 195). In many cases, what were formerly "productivity" projects are now redescribed (or repackaged) as "quality" efforts. Many of these, such as dramatic improvements in vehicle maintenance at the New York City Department of Sanitation, were described as "productivity" improvements prior to the TQM movement.

The Local Government Information Network (LOGIN, 1997) database, for example, contains more than 650 examples of programs with a quality component dating back through the 1980s. In 1993, West, Berman, and Milakovich estimated "that twenty-six percent of all cities over 25,000 population used TQM in at least one functional area . . . most often police work, parks and recreation services, personnel management, and budgetary reporting" (p. 179).

While not new then, quality management has become a fundamental element of the reinventing government movement. Just as the private sector is shifting from bureaucratic to customer-responsive management approaches in order to remain competitive in a global marketplace, government is becoming more quality conscious to meet the challenges posed by privatization and to meet the public's view of itself as customers, deserving of the highest-quality services.

NOTE

▪
_____

1. Unfortunately these volumes (Vol. 1. Introduction; Vol. 2. How to Get Started; Vol. 3. Appendix to #1; Vol. 4. Education and Training), as well as the very comprehensive *Federal TQM Documents Catalog and Database User Guide* (with several hundred entries), are no longer available because the Federal Quality Institute was terminated during a series of recent budget cuts.

REFERENCES

▪
_____

Cohen, S., & Brand, R. (1993). *Total quality management in government: A practical guide for the real world.* San Francisco: Jossey-Bass.

Deming, W. E. (1986). *Out of the crisis.* Cambridge: MIT Center for Advanced Engineering Study.

Hunt, D. V. (1993). *Quality management for government.* Milwaukee, WI: ASQC Quality Press.

Hyde, A. C. (1992). The proverbs of total quality management: Recharting the path to quality improvement in the public sector. *Public Productivity and Management Review, 16*(1), 25-37.

Juran, J. M. (1988). *Juran on leadership for quality.* New York: McGraw-Hill.

LOGIN (Local government information network). (1997). [Computer database]. St. Paul, MN: Norris Institute.

Milakovich, M. E. (1992). Total quality management for public service productivity improvement. In M. Holzer (Ed.), *Public productivity handbook* (pp. 577-602). New York: Marcel Dekker.

Mizaur, D. (1993). Quality government is government of the people, by the people, for the people. *Public Productivity and Management Review, 16(4), Summer, 12pp.*

Poister, T. H. (1992). Productivity monitoring: Systems, indicators, and analysis. In M. Holzer (Ed.), *Public productivity handbook* (pp. 195-212). New York: Marcel Dekker.

U.S. Federal Quality Institute. (FQI). (1990). *Total quality management in the federal government* (4 vols.). Washington, DC: U.S. Federal Quality Institute, U.S. Office of Personnel Management.

U.S. General Accounting Office. (1991). *Management practices—U.S. companies improve performance through quality efforts* (GAO/NSIAD-91-190, May). Washington, DC: Government Printing Office.

U.S. General Accounting Office. (1992). *Quality management—Survey of federal organizations* (GAO/GGD-93-9BR, October). Washington, DC: Government Printing Office.

West, J. P., Berman, E. M., & Milakovich, M. E. (1993). Implementing TQM in local government: The leadership challenge. *Public Productivity and Management Review, 17*(2).

3

HUMAN RESOURCE MANAGEMENT

■

```
┌─────────────────────────────────────┐
│       Developing Human Resources     │
└─────────────────────────────────────┘
```

Recruiting the Best and Brightest —
Providing Systematic Training —
Recognizing Diversity —
Building Services by Building Teams —
Providing Employee Assistance —
Balancing Employee and Organizational Needs —

PEOPLE AND PRODUCTIVITY
■

Quality management requires public sector managers who are willing to rethink human resource management. In a society with higher, quality-oriented expectations, the traditional bureaucratic, hierarchical management style is insufficient. Yet too many organizations, public and private, fail to utilize or maintain intelligently their expensive human capital. The reason for this is simple: It is difficult and it takes a lot of time and effort. The easiest way to increase productivity, in the short run, may be to introduce new technology or mechanize a process. However, the more

49

enduring, but more difficult, way to improve productivity is to develop each worker's individual capacity and desire to function at the highest level possible.

EXSL awardees provide evidence that, in practice, "people approaches" are just as important as procedural, fiscal, or technological factors in improving productivity and the quality of services provided. Virtually all of the EXSL recipients recognize that productivity is dependent upon people who deal with clients, operate equipment, enter data, and solve unanticipated problems. People are the foundation upon which the successes of every public organization rest.

The enlightened management of human resources is particularly important in the public sector because government's most extensive and expensive investments are people; most public organizations devote from 50% to 85% of their budgets to employee salaries and benefits. Because those "human resources" have complicated needs, responsive public organizations have adopted enlightened human resource practices, rejecting an authoritarian, bureaucratic style. Public organizations have often recognized that a productive organization is humane, structured around not only the task but its members and their human needs. They understand that the art of leadership inheres in getting people to work well for the organization by grasping and responding to their needs.

MULTIPLE MOTIVATORS

Typically, EXSL awardees use the full range of state-of-the-art approaches to motivating and managing employees:

■ They recognize that motivation requires management of many interrelated elements. Ban, Faerman, and Riccucci (1992) hold that to achieve their goals, public organizations need to take an integrated approach to personnel management, linking workforce planning, recruitment, hiring, training, and other personnel policies. Building and maintaining a productive workforce includes (a) developing a formal workforce plan, (b) actively recruiting job applicants, (c) redesigning tests or developing creative alternatives to written tests, (d) linking training and development activities to organizational mission, and (e) revising personnel policies to meet the needs of employees.

■ They understand that money can be an important motivator, but is not the only motivational option. A sense of being able to make a difference in the organization is more important to the job satisfaction of public sector managers than to that of private managers (Balfour & Wechsler, 1991).

■ They apply performance appraisal systems. Daly (1992) points out that productivity is a function of motivation, and motivation—extrinsic or intrinsic—is itself a function of the recognition of an individual's work effort. Such recognition can come from a well-conceived and well-managed system of performance appraisal.

■ They develop integrated, mutually reinforcing processes. Guy (1992) points out that many interdependent factors contribute to creating a productive work environment: an organizational culture that relies on such factors as team building, maximizing the strengths of employees while compensating for their weaknesses, open communication channels, flexibility in the midst of predictability, and balancing the needs of the organization with the needs of employees.

West and Berman (1995) identify four forces that emphasize the need for innovations in human resource development:

1. *The Changing Composition of the Workforce.* Ban and colleagues (1992), Bruce and Olshfski (1993), and Johnston and Packer (1987) present a broad array of challenges to the public sector based upon the increasing diversity of the workforce. For example, many people are entering the workforce without the appropriate skills and training, and these deficiencies adversely affect their career advancement potential as well as their organization's effectiveness (Kleeman, 1992; VanWart, Cayer, & Cook, 1993).

2. *Changing Nature of Public Sector Jobs.* Many public sector jobs require increased skill and education levels; therefore, the public sector will have to invest in training. Surveys of local government managers indicate that many future jobs will rely on advanced technology (Woolridge & Webster, 1991), yet these demands come at a time when resources are stretched and budgets limited. Training dollars are typically the first to go (Gordon, 1991).

3. *Declining Prestige of Public Sector Jobs.* Many qualified candidates are not attracted to careers in the public sector. It follows that government

needs to work constantly to improve the image of the public sector and needs to make recruitment efforts targeted to recent graduates, victims of downsizing, and older employees with experience.

4. Increasing Organizational Effectiveness. Training and development activities are needed to enable managers and employees to "reinvent themselves" and to build "high-performance" workplaces (Osborne & Gaebler, 1992). "As governments invest in 'human capital' and become learning centers, it is more likely that they will harness and channel the energy of the public workforce and promote high-performance workplaces" (West & Berman, 1995, p. 86).

We have found that, rather than taking a simple-minded, out-of-date approach to the management of complex human assets, EXSL awardees confirm the type of multidimensional approach that Guy, West, Berman, and others suggest. They are systematically addressing the contemporary problems of human resource management.

They recognize that productive management begins with human resources:

1. recruiting appropriate human resources, paid or volunteer, and
2. developing and maintaining those resources through systematic training.

Then they create a high performance workforce by

3. recognizing the diversity of their workforce, and
4. providing comprehensive employee assistance when needed, and

they facilitate the production of services by

5. balancing organizational and employee interests, and
6. building teams.

RECRUITING THE BEST AND BRIGHTEST

To provide high-quality, responsive service to their citizens, government agencies must hire highly talented and skilled public servants. Thus, personnel recruitment—the very beginning of the system of human resource management—is both a problem and an opportunity that the most forward-looking jurisdictions have recognized and addressed. They begin by attracting the very best people to public sector careers.

Hiring the Highly Skilled. Under the *Innovations in Recruiting and Hiring* program, Wisconsin state government provides responsive service to government agencies seeking to hire highly skilled public servants. The hiring innovations pioneered by the Department of Employment Relations provide a package of more efficient, responsive, and "user-friendly" civil service hiring systems. These innovations—the Entry-Level Professional Program, the Critical Recruitment Program, Walk-In Civil Service Testing, and JOBS (Job Opportunity Bulletin System)—have greatly enhanced the state's ability to hire employees who are both highly qualified and reflect the state's diversity:

- The Entry-Level Professional Program (EPP) and Critical Recruitment Program (CRP) both use creative alternatives to the written multiple-choice exams still used in most jurisdictions, alternatives that are more user-friendly, impose fewer bureaucratic hurdles on applicants, minimize disparate impact, and enable hiring decisions to be based on specific qualifications, not just "book knowledge."
- Walk-In Testing eliminates bureaucratic barriers in cases in which multiple-choice exams are still most appropriate. In these cases, applicants simply "walk-in" to testing centers, apply immediately, and take exams. Although other jurisdictions may use walk-in testing on a limited basis, Wisconsin is the only state to use walk-in testing as its exclusive written testing method.
- JOBS provides immediate, broad access to vacancy announcements throughout Wisconsin. Applicants no longer have to depend solely on printed, mailed copies of announcements. Now, they simply dial in to a statewide system and access up-to-date information.

The overall goal of these innovations—which are more flexible and accessible than traditional civil service hiring procedures—is to enable Wisconsin to attract and hire the talented people needed to provide the best possible services to its citizens. That goal has been achieved by systematically creating hiring systems that are timely, easy for applicants to understand and compete within, and provide managers with greater hiring choices. Just as important, they adhere to the fairness and merit principles fundamental to civil service. This innovation anticipated the National Commission on the State and Local Public Service's recommendation to "end civil service paralysis" by reforming hiring systems.

Searching for Executives. The state of Washington also received EXSL recognition for its top-level recruitment model. The Executive Search Services, the public sector equivalent of a private sector search firm, effectively designs and carries out methods for identifying, screening, interviewing, and ultimately hiring top-level executives for state government. The program designs and leads nationwide searches for director, deputy director, and assistant director positions. Managed and staffed by state employees, the service's main purpose is to provide quality public sector executive recruitment expertise. Executive search services are available to any state agency, board, commission, or institution of higher education. In addition, the program provides services to public sector entities such as cities, counties, port districts, other states, and the federal government. Funded on a "charge-back" basis, it provides those services at only one fifth of the national average cost of using a private search firm for comparable services.

Recruiting Volunteers. Under increasing fiscal pressure and increased demands for citizen services, governments are also recruiting unpaid volunteers. Many people who work with government are volunteers who enable agencies to stretch limited resources by facilitating and complementing the efforts of paid personnel. Traditional volunteers within the public sector include auxiliary police, volunteer firefighters, ambulance drivers, teacher and library aides, and hospital auxiliary members. In Texas, the Department of Human Services (TDHS) added to that traditional list by establishing a *Volunteer Interpreter Service (VIS).* Faced with the need to service an increasingly diverse population of non-English-speaking residents, the TDHS introduced the VIS service in order to ameliorate a language barrier between staff and non-English-speaking applicants for food stamps, Medicaid, and Aid to Families with Dependent Children. Communication problems created errors in work, disrupted service, and required an inordinate amount of time. But now volunteers are available to interpret, either in person or by phone, in more than 20 different languages, reflecting those that staff hear most often, including Vietnamese, Spanish, Russian, and Kurdish. Staff members also have access to an automated resource directory containing the volunteers' names, phone numbers, and times of availability. The volunteer interpreters include community members with disabilities, college students, mothers at home with children, clients enrolled in job skills training courses, and community members trying to help people of their own culture.

In Visalia, California, more than 2,000 volunteers donated over 200,000 hours of services to city agencies and community organizations; their time is valued at more than one million dollars. The *Volunteer Service Program (VSP)* is the consolidation of all the existing volunteer programs in Visalia into one coordinated program that combines the efforts of the Retired Senior Volunteer Services Program (RSVP), the Young Volunteers in Action, and the Volunteer Center. In addition, VSP is responsible for recruiting volunteers for all official city committees and advisory boards.

The consolidation of volunteer efforts not only increased the effectiveness and visibility of the volunteer initiatives, but it also decreased the costs associated with providing volunteers. VSP serves 115 government and community service agencies providing volunteer job development services, volunteer recruitment and screening, and training on how to use volunteers effectively. VSP also developed a supervisor's handbook to complement the training workshops.

Some of the biggest savings to the city result from volunteers in the finance department who open the mail, research and file the records, and assist in collecting community taxes. Volunteers who help sort tax bills and receipts have been able to process bank deposits more quickly and earn the public more than $130,000 a year in additional interest. In addition, volunteers in the tax department actively enforce the city's business tax, correlating records and finding accounts that were not being taxed.

PROVIDING SYSTEMATIC TRAINING

Recruitment is only the first step in improving an organization's capacity to deliver services. Effective team efforts also require effective, ongoing training, a factor that EXSL has recognized in several programs. Several EXSL best practice awardees have developed responsible models for the next step: helping prepare employees to perform.

Training the Trainers. In Illinois, the *Training Information Resource Center (TIRC)* provides cost-effective training to the 3,000 employees of the Illinois Department of Employment Security. TIRC offers custom training based upon employees' participation in curriculum development: individual employees or groups of employees of the Illinois Department of

Employment Security identify technical training needs rather than have training thrust upon them. TIRC then trains pools of employees to serve as trainers for other employees, and those individuals may borrow books, videotapes, and audio cassettes for home study. The program is effective in providing timely, cost-effective, high quality training: a 4-person staff produced training results that previously eluded a 22-person staff, and local office managers report that productivity is up.

Preparing for Emergencies. As one of the leading chemical producing states in the nation, New Jersey designed a training program in response to a clear and urgent need to ensure that public sector employees are prepared to respond quickly, efficiently, and effectively in the event of a release of a hazardous substance. After closely reviewing federal standards and OSHA legislation, the Hazardous Material Emergency Response Planning Unit of the New Jersey State Police developed a statewide program in conjunction with local emergency response teams. The objective is to minimize potential injuries and deaths associated with chemical spills, and the means of accomplishing that objective is to ensure a safe, professional response to hazardous material incidents. The *Hazardous Material Training Program* creates, maintains, and administers training courses in hazardous materials response that comply with or exceed quality standards established under state mandate. Courses are developed in a modular format to accommodate students' availability. The program is widely accepted in the emergency response community and is highly regarded as a standardized training curriculum throughout the state. The unit also maintains a computerized registration database and certificate-issuance system for the state's 120,000 public sector emergency responders.

Licensing Providers. The *Caring for Kids Neighborhood Day Care Home Project* in Jacksonville, Florida, is a collaborative neighborhood day care effort to increase options for welfare recipients. It helps them to attain permanent self-sufficiency by becoming licensed family day care home providers, resulting in savings of $11,000 per recipient in welfare payments. Not only does the project train welfare recipients and offer them the opportunity to become self-sufficient, but the state saves approximately $11,000 a year for each recipient who successfully takes part in the training program. In addition, the newly trained day care providers fill a need for low-income families—affordable child care conveniently located in their neighborhoods.

Jacksonville, Florida, has some 10,000 Aid to Families with Dependent Children (AFDC) recipients. It is estimated that there are at least 50,000 children who are 13 years of age or younger and in need of day care. The Caring for Kids project addresses the issues of long-term unemployment, welfare dependency, inadequate job skills, insufficient educational training, and an inadequate supply of neighborhood home day care services.

Interested welfare recipients have the option of becoming licensed family day care home providers, which assists them in achieving economic self-sufficiency. This innovative project provides a variety of classroom assignments and real-life work experience opportunities for the participants. It also provides support services for the participants, such as transportation and child care. Caring for Kids is funded by the City of Jacksonville, and guarantees that each participant, upon successful completion of the program, receives a child care subcontract worth $13,000-$15,000 annually. Through the partnership between the city and the private sector, the program has been able to provide welfare recipients with a meaningful occupation, thus building a sense of pride and dignity. It has been able to lower unemployment, has saved welfare payments, and provides additional day care capability in the low-income areas where it is most needed.

RECOGNIZING DIVERSITY

Although service delivery is often dependent on cooperation among service providers, valuable contributions by personnel eager to solve problems are often stifled by the problems of discrimination and bias.

Valuing Differences. The city of San Diego has a long history of successful recruitment and hiring of women and people of color into the system. Until 1992, however, the city was not as successful in addressing their needs, such as providing support systems and equitable policies, once they joined the organization.

San Diego was recognized by EXSL for its *Diversity Commitment,* a proactive citywide effort to be responsive to the diversity within the workforce and dedicated to changing the way all employees are viewed, valued, and treated. The diversity effort was launched by the City Manager's Office to frame diversity as a strategic direction and future resource. The goal is to create an environment in which differences are valued, and all city employees are a productive part of a high-performing team delivering services to a community of more than 2 million people. It is a long-term and strategic plan that includes data gathering and discussion, ongoing education, problem solving, and changes in systemwide policies and procedures.

Through this program, the city is uncovering and reducing the "isms" (e.g., sexism, racism, heterosexism) inherent in the policies and behaviors that impact agency effectiveness and productivity. Over 200 qualitative and quantitative changes have occurred in the way business is done, people are treated, and policies are carried out.

PROVIDING EMPLOYEE ASSISTANCE

Employees often suffer crises in their personal lives. Needing medical care, addiction, marital crises, abuse, and financial stress are only examples of the stresses that may overflow into the workplace, impinging on productivity. Enlightened, high-performing organizations recognize that relatively small investments in helping employees overcome those problems will improve employee morale and loyalty and, just as important, result in substantial savings or cost avoidances to the organization.

Assisting Employees. In 1988, the City of Memphis, Tennessee, launched an *Employee Assistance Program* (EAP) in response to estimated losses of $3,500,000 per year in reduced efficiency, absenteeism, and accidents as a result of untreated personal problems and disorders. The city established a broad-based effort designed to address various counseling, rehabilitation, and crisis-intervention needs. Currently, more than 1,000 employees and their families participate in the program, which has as its goal the improvement of efficiency, productivity, attendance, health, and the overall quality of life of its municipal employees and their families.

The *Employee Assistance Program* significantly reduced losses by at least 25% through the implementation of employee education programs, training, union participation, and a modification in health care benefits. One of the target concerns of the program is the creation of a drug-free environment. To date, the program has succeeded in reducing medical care expenditures for substance abuse by half. In addition, a set of follow-up procedures has been established to track employees with problems of impaired performance, attendance, or both. Through this effort, at-risk employees can be quickly identified, and intervention can take place before the problems reach critical levels. The EAP is cost-effective: For every dollar spent in EAP, four dollars are returned in reduced health care costs and improved efficiency and attendance. The City enhances its EAP by offering a unique range of services to its employees, including referral to non-hospital-based treatment programs, intensive follow-up procedures, and the careful match of employee to individualized substance abuse programs.

A similar employee assistance effort in the state of California was also recognized with an EXSL award. The *Employee Assistance Program* in Buena Park provides in-house counseling to municipal employees coping with such problems as stress, alcohol and drug abuse, family and marital crisis, job problems, child and spousal abuse, and money and credit management problems. This unique and innovative program for small city government provides a holistic approach to meeting the personal needs of the city employee. The program is provided and managed in-house by the city psychologist for all types of crisis intervention. As they enter the system, efforts are also made to assess potential employees through psychological screenings and then to continue their development both personally and professionally through exposure to the in-service training program, "Investment in Excellence." The variety of problems receiving attention include: family and marital crisis, stress, alcohol and drug dependency, job problems, child and spousal abuse, legal problems, care of and issues relating to elderly or infirm relatives, death and dying, and money and credit management.

The introduction of EAP led to significant cost savings. Prior to EAP the city psychologist worked in crisis intervention with the city police department. A vehicle for handling the general employee population problems did not exist. Consequently, problems with employee absenteeism due to accidents and illness were rising. EAP addresses this problem, and since its introduction the program has been directly or partly responsible for more than $2 million in savings, particularly through a 75% reduction in disability retirements.

Although most agencies this size have traditionally "contracted out" their EAP services under the assumption that up-front per-employee cost usually appears lower, this program demonstrates that a smaller agency can have an in-house program and can save considerably more money in doing so.

BUILDING SERVICES BY BUILDING TEAMS

EXSL recognizes teams, not individuals, and awardees consistently recognize that more productive services are achieved not by isolated individuals working alone and competing against each other, but by teams working cooperatively and supporting their colleagues. Thus, awardees often build programs that maximize the strengths of employees while compensating for their weaknesses.

Sharing Savings. The *Shared Savings Program (SSP)* of Pittsburg, California, is the culmination of the Public Services Department's 10-year effort to build private-sector-type performance incentives into municipal public works employment as an effort to cut costs while increasing productivity. The program links employee compensation with efficient utilization of equipment, supplies, and labor resources. The result of this venture is that Pittsburg's employees have grown to appreciate the value of city property and materials while significantly reducing the cost of public works services.

The SSP features increased employee involvement in generating work standards, performance targets, and work scheduling. It combines productivity incentives with such tools as "Deficiency Notices" in order to encourage employee teams to place increased attention on cutting costs and increasing both the quality and quantity of public service. The Shared Savings Program works as follows:

1. Participants in the program are selected by their peers.
2. All funds that the personnel have direct control of are pooled in a single fund.
3. The group has its own accountant to log all costs on a daily basis.
4. All materials and supplies, repairs, and the like, along with salaries, are charged to the account.
5. Quality is controlled by a deficiency notice, which places a financial penalty against the group's account. Individual deficiencies do not exceed $200.
6. Savings (coming in under budget) are split 60/40 with shares going to the employees and city, respectively.

As a result of this program, the unit cost of maintenance services has been reduced in meter reading from 78 cents to 33 cents per unit; one individual now reads all water meters in only 120 hours per month, versus 1.5 individuals over some 240 hours per month it took previously.

The results in the street sweeping program are also significant, with costs falling from $15 to $10 per curb mile swept, cutting 40% per month off the time previously required for this work. The unit compensation program in janitorial services has reduced costs significantly (the last "low" private sector bidder came in $32,000 above the city's crew). The SSP in park maintenance was responsible for an estimated $60,000 of savings in its first year of operation, at the same time that there was an appreciable improvement in the quality of services provided.

BALANCING EMPLOYEE
AND ORGANIZATIONAL NEEDS

Classical management concepts often assume a tension between employee and employer. Tight rules, systems, and supervision are necessary to limit counterproductive indiscretion, dishonesty, and laziness. Employees view the organization as an enemy, and vice versa; work is merely an interruption in their leisure time, and a great deal of energy is wasted attempting to sidestep those constraints. Organizations can be minimally productive under such assumptions, but almost never produce at high levels of productivity and quality. Rather, organizations that work at high levels also work as partners with their employees. They recognize that burdensome rules, avoidable travel, and unavoidable health problems or personal stress all limit performance.

Freeing Managers From Excessive Rules. At the middle management level, the state of Washington streamlined its middle management personnel system to allow some 2,500 such managers to operate more productively. Members of this group retain the protections of the civil service system, but are covered by a separate set of personnel rules that emphasize flexibility, decentralization, and individual accountability. The *Management Service* does away with traditional civil service standards, such as job classifications, recruitment registers, and salary ranges. Instead, a point factor evaluation system is used to place each position into one of four broad management bands, which provide parameters for salary determination.

Telecommuting/Telework. A regional mandate to downsize local government by managing human resources and office space more effectively prompted Los Angeles County to introduce a *Telecommuting Program*. The primary objective of this program is to promote a more productive work-at-home or near-home work option for employees who commute long distances to their work places. The secondary objective was to meet a regional mandate to downsize local government by managing human resources and office space more efficiently. Both of these objectives enable the county to meet regional environmental regulations of the Clean Air Act.

Labor representatives were consulted, and a telecommuting agreement was negotiated outlining employer/employee responsibilities. The agreement is supported by behavior change and workplace alternatives training models. More than 4,000 employees in Los Angeles County telecommute an average of 1.5 days a week. Through a reduction in sick leave and overtime, the county has realized a 10% increase in productivity and $13 million in annual savings. Over 144,000 hours of travel time and more than 73 tons of air pollutants have been eliminated annually. Employee costs savings were also high. Personal expenses related to commuting—such as car operation and maintenance—as well as personal expenses related to central office work behavior were reduced an average of $720 annually. In addition, the use of telecommuting as a workplace emergency response initiative enabled the county to keep county services available to clients immediately following the Northridge earthquake in 1994.

Labor-Management Cooperation. The key to a successful partnership is a collaborative labor relations program based on mutual trust and respect. Marion County, Oregon, and its largest union developed such a partnership—negotiating wages and benefits within a cap on the employer's future expenditures. The *Model for Capping Wage and Benefit Expenditures* defines the employer's maximum future personnel service costs while giving the union flexibility to bargain changes in salaries, insurance, and other employee benefits.

The county faced voter-mandated property tax reform that threatened the stability of future county revenues. For budgeting purposes, the county sought a way to place a total cap on its annual personnel expenses while recognizing the union's need to obtain a reasonable wage and benefit package for its employees. The jointly developed model achieves both objectives while enhancing mutual trust and respect through a collaborative bargaining process.

Specifically, Marion County negotiated a 3-year labor contract with an economic reopener in the 2nd and 3rd years. Contract language allows the union the right to bargain on the cost and type of benefits, including its cost-of-living adjustment (COLA). However, the total annualized cost to the county for all wages, benefits, and "related payroll costs" was not to exceed 6% for the succeeding year. This model also creates an incentive for employees to control their use of health, dental, and worker's compensation benefits. Employees thus influence their COLA or are able to purchase additional benefits by decreasing the cost of insurance. The employees are rewarded for decreasing these costs while the county's total personnel costs remain fixed. The employer can project wage and benefit costs for budgeting purposes prior to the completion of the negotiations on the economic components of the labor contract.

Providing Affordable Health Insurance. In the State of New Hampshire, The *Hanover Health Plan* provides a unique delivery of health insurance by combining a high-deductible plan at a reasonable price with a trust fund to pool or share the risk of the deductibles. The old health plan combined high-quality coverage with convenience, a very appealing program that created formidable resistance to change. The new plan, which saves $800+ per family membership and $230+ per individual membership per year, is less convenient only in terms of out-of-pocket costs and paperwork. Filling out insurance forms is not a popular sport, but employees felt that the inconvenience was worth the savings of $800 per year.

CONCLUSION

In pursuit of performance, government's best practices suggest a set of typical people-oriented diagnostic questions that should be asked by and of managers:

■ Can employees have a voice in decisions that affect them? These might include joint labor-management committees, quality circles, or vertically integrated problem-solving task forces.

■ Does management create an environment that workers feel part of? Indicators of a participatory, fear-free workplace are open information, open doors, and an atmosphere in which risk takers are not punished for the inevitable failures.

■ Are people involved in looking for improvement opportunities? Employees are often the first, best (and cheapest) sources for identifying barriers and obstacles to overcome, tasks to be done more efficiently, work that might be dropped, shortened or simplified, and so on.

■ Are employees challenged by work that uses their skills, abilities, and intelligence? Most employees feel they can operate at higher levels of responsibility and are willing to do so if given appropriate opportunities. Appropriate training should be available to upgrade skills and enhance knowledge.

■ Does management provide support and assistance to employees coping with problems? A "yes" to this question presumes that managers and employees are adequately trained, adequately equipped, and adequately informed.

To the extent these questions are answered, public servants will be more efficient and effective, agencies will deliver promised services, and citizens will find that their workforce is a valuable, productive asset.

REFERENCES

Balfour, D. L., & Wechsler, B. (1991). Commitment, performance, and productivity in public organizations. *Public Productivity and Management Review, 15*(1), 355-368.

Ban, C., Faerman, S. R., & Riccucci, N. (1992). Productivity and the personnel process. In M. Holzer (Ed.), *Public productivity handbook* (pp. 401-423). New York: Marcel Dekker.

Bruce, W., & Olshfski, D. (1993). The new American workplace. In M. Holzer (Ed.), *Public productivity handbook* (pp. 425-443). New York: Marcel Dekker.

Daly, D. M. (1992). Pay for performance, performance appraisal, and total quality management. *Public Productivity and Management Review, 16*(2), 39-52.

Gordon, J. (1991). Training budgets: Recessions take a bite. *Training, 28*(10), 37-45.

Guy, M. E. (1992). Productive work environment. In M. Holzer (Ed.), *Public productivity handbook* (pp. 321-335). New York: Marcel Dekker.

Johnston, W., & Packer, R. (1987). *Workforce 2000: Work and workers for the 21st century.* Indianapolis: Hudson Institute.

Kleeman, R. (1992). *The changing workforce: Demographic issues facing the federal government.* Washington, DC: Government Accounting Office.

Osborne, D., & Gaebler, T. (1992). *Reinventing government.* Reading, MA: Addison-Wesley.

VanWart, M., Cayer, N. J., & Cook, S. (1993). *Handbook of training and development for the public sector.* San Francisco: Jossey-Bass.

West, J. P., & Berman, E. M. (1995). Strategic human resource and career planning. In S. W. Hayes & R. C. Kearney (Eds.), *Public personnel administration: Problems and prospects* (3rd ed., pp. 73-88). Englewood Cliffs, NJ: Prentice Hall.

Woolridge, B., & Wester, J. (1991). The turbulent environment of public personnel administration: Responding to the challenge of the changing workplace of the twenty-first century. *Public Personnel Management, 20*(2), 207-224.

ADAPTING
TECHNOLOGY

Adapting Technology

Providing Open Access to Data —
Automation for Enhanced Productivity —
Delivering on the Public's Demands —
Cost-Effective Applications —
Cross-Cutting Techniques —

GOVERNMENT-AS-INVENTOR

Motivated, trained employees are only part of the productivity and quality improvement "formula." Each individual needs to be supported by reliable, up-to-date technologies. Advanced technologies are as important to the public as to the private sector. Both sectors need powerful computer and information systems, automated and rapid communications, energy-saving and security-enhancing devices, and an almost limitless menu of "hardware and software." To meet these needs, government often relies on off-the-shelf products developed by the private sector.

But when adequate products are not available, the public sector has taken the initiative to pioneer new systems. Government employees have invented lasers, solid state technology, the basic design of most commercial and military aircraft, instrument landing systems, the first modern computer, titanium (and other stronger and lighter materials), the CAT scan, plastic corneas, advanced fishing nets, nuclear power, Teflon, wash-and-wear fabrics, resuscitation devices, and plastic wrap (Public Employees Roundtable, 1987-1997).

Profiting from government's large up-front investments in such products, business has brought these products to the market. NASA (1996), for example, has a continuing program to help the private sector exploit innovations resulting from the space program. Sometimes government shares in those profits through licensing or royalty arrangements. Typically, however, the public sector and public servants receive neither royalties nor sufficient recognition.

Technologies that make possible improved performance are not limited to high-tech or computer applications. They apply to roads and sewers as much as they do to satellites and smart bombs. In as mundane an area as refuse collection, for example, departments of sanitation in New York City, Scottsdale, Arizona, and other localities have developed and applied productive technological changes, sometimes patenting those innovations:

- Trucks designed specifically for operation by two men, rather than the traditional three-man team
- Remote-control arms that allow the driver to lift and empty large containers of refuse
- Robotic truck painters, which a management-labor team approached the private sector to design
- Tire-changing machines designed specifically to the agency's standards and intended to alleviate the high degree of manual work in the operation
- Purchase of "high dump" street cleaning brooms, which are faster, safer, and can dump refuse into another vehicle
- Redesign of the equipment used to transport refuse from barges to landfills

The development and adaptation of technology for applied problem solving is often initiated by local or state governments. It is also a function of deliberate, goal-oriented efforts. Public Technology, Inc., for example, is devoted to the development and diffusion of productive technologies for state and local government.

EXSL award winners utilize technology to improve services to the public through four overlapping approaches:

- Providing open access to data by citizens and businesses
- Automating programs to improve efficiency
- Providing improved, higher-quality services to the public
- Operating programs more cost-effectively

Although most technology-oriented EXSL awardees emphasize one of these four, some made comprehensive efforts that represent a fifth emphasis:

- Cross-cutting techniques

PROVIDING OPEN ACCESS TO DATA

One obstacle to effective government, as well as to confidence in government, is lack of access to information. Citizens and businesses are often frustrated, angered, and alienated by difficulties in obtaining necessary information as to eligibility, deadlines, status, demographics, and more.

Equal Electronic Access. In 1990, the Kansas legislature enacted the Information Network of Kansas Act. The resulting *Information Network of Kansas (INK)* breaks down barriers to nonconfidential information by providing on-line computer access to public information maintained by state, county, and local government entities. INK's mission is to provide equal electronic access to public information to the citizens of Kansas. People become exceedingly frustrated when, as they try to obtain information from state agencies, they are placed on hold or transferred from department to department. Many citizens give up on accessing information they are interested in due to the fragmentation of state government and the frustration they experience. Through a cooperative effort on the part of government agencies, corporate executives, and private citizens, INK strives to make public information accessible. INK is a comprehensive response that alleviates citizen frustration and addresses the need to access public information easily.

In its first year of operation, INK attracted more than 2,000 subscribers accessing 83 on-line applications consisting of over 100 separate information sources within Kansas state, county, and local government. Free access is available to all citizens in public libraries and in multimedia kiosks in many supermarkets and shopping centers. INK is supported entirely through a minimal per-minute fee charged to businesses within the state that access the system to obtain necessary documents and permits. As a result, INK is 100% fee funded and has neither requested nor received public appropriations, grants, or subsidies of any kind.

Open Government. In the same spirit of open government, the Texas State Comptroller's *Window on State Government* bulletin board system (BBS) was developed by the comptroller's Research and Application Systems Divisions in an effort to distribute data and information more widely to citizens of the state. As the principal tax administrator and chief fiscal officer for the state, one of the comptroller's functions is to compile and maintain tax and economic data. The comptroller's office receives thousands of data requests from individuals, companies, and government agencies throughout the state, and the agency faced the challenge of distributing this data in a timely, cost-effective manner.

As part of the comptroller's strategic plan, one of the agency's primary goals is to "maximize customer service satisfaction by improving services while minimizing administrative burdens on those we serve." In keeping with the comptroller's philosophy of "open government," the BBS enables government to be more responsive to the citizens of the state.

Using an 800 number, citizens may dial in to the electronic bulletin board system to access data and download files to personal computers. The system is operational 24 hours a day, 7 days a week. Some of the data accessed by citizens include the following:

- Gross and retail sales by city, county, and metro area
- Employment data by region and metro area
- Texas economic indicators
- Texas population forecast
- Local allocation data by city
- State spending by category and year
- State revenue by source
- Policy Research and Exchange Program
- Statewide elected officials and legislators

- State and Federal Grant Directory
- State Purchasing and Historically Underutilized Business (HUB) program
- Text of the NAFTA and National Performance Review

Window on State Government also allows users to connect to other Texas government BBSs, free of charge. Some of the dial-out options include: Texas Department of Commerce: "Texas Marketplace"; Texas Employment Commission; Texas Parks & Wildlife Department: "The Outdoor BBS"; Texas Ethics Commission; Office of the Governor; "Texas Victims Assistance Network"; and the Texas Cancer Council.

Remote Access. In the state of Utah, *Datashare* provides similar direct computer access services to all of Utah's corporation, registration, and commercial code records on file with the Division of Corporations and Commercial Code. This division is the equivalent of the secretary of state's office found in most states. Datashare, the only system of its kind in the United States at the time, provides unrestricted search capabilities by a business name, a person's name, federal tax ID number, and Standard Industrial Code.

As a means of facilitating commerce, this central registry of business records is in constant use by the public, law firms, financial institutions, tax agencies, and law enforcement groups to identify business ownership, UCC debtor/credit status, and legal liabilities for businesses and corporations. Datashare can be accessed 24 hours a day, 7 days a week, for a monthly user fee of $25 plus 30 cents per on-line minute.

Prior to Datashare, the division staff was faced with growing demands for services and the state legislature had refused to increase the division's budget and staff.

- The division was responding to over 400,000 telephone inquiries, each for simple record information. Callers were on hold an average of 15 minutes before being served.
- Processing formal record searches took up to 5 business days.
- Processing new documents for filing took up to 10 business days.

With more than 1,200 users, Datashare has

- Reduced processing turn-around time for new filings from 10 days to 5 minutes

- Implemented immediate record searches in contrast to the previous typical delay of 5 days
- Reduced the telephone inquires workload from nearly 400,000 per year to less than 230,000
- Allowed staff to devote more time to quality customer service

An overwhelming response to Datashare allowed it to "pay for itself" in under 3 years, less time than originally estimated to save the legislatively appropriated funding, and the early repayment of the funding enabled the state to reduce Datashare user fees. With the advent of Datashare, new service opportunities became possible, such as one-stop business service centers, providing business registration services and information, state tax filings and services, and even IRS information.

Competition Through Computerization. In Oregon, computers are used to enhance the purchasing and bidding process for state goods and services. In an effort to increase competition and lower costs, the state of Oregon implemented the first automated bid access system in the country. The Oregon *Vendor Information Program (VIP)* allows vendors to use an IBM-compatible personal computer and modem to access current and historical bid information 24 hours a day, 7 days a week. Vendors can view and download purchasing information in the convenience of their own home or office. Easy access fundamentally changes the way the state of Oregon procures products, trade services, and public works. VIP replaced 50 years of public purchasing procedures that were encumbered with a labor-intensive, cost-prohibitive paper bid distribution system.

Prior to January 1992, requests for proposals (RFPs) were handled in Oregon as they are in most places: Vendors registered with the state, then periodically received fat RFPs in the mail. Postage costs alone were $144,000 per year. Vendors now use modem-equipped personal computers, or those in libraries, community colleges, and local chambers of commerce, to call the state's Vendor Information System computer. They can register on-line, download the appropriate RFPs, and have access to historical information such as who won the bid last time, who lost, and the amounts of the winning and losing bids.

The entire system cost less than $400,000, mostly for the IBM computer and public relations effort to sell this new way of doing business to the vendor community. Staff reductions and postage savings paid for the system within the first year. In the first five quarters after the system went on-line, state officials say they realized more than $17 million in savings on the same products that had been purchased under the old system. The reason: competition. Not only are more vendors bidding for state business—instant access to RFPs has increased the number of bidding vendors by one third—but the historical information available to them on similar previous contracts has improved the quality of the bids. With the old way of doing business, three or four bids would be submitted for a contract and there would be a wide margin between the quotes. According to the Director of Purchasing, "Price quotes were all over the board, but with VIP, the bids are right on target and very competitive."

VIP is a work in progress. The purchasing division plans to market the program to local governments, allowing them to put their RFPs on the state system for a small fee. And purchasing officials are trying to improve the system by allowing vendors to submit their bids on-line. Unfortunately, while vendors can download RFPs, they cannot upload their bids to the state, because bids are still required to be signed in ink. An act of legislation is necessary to change that requirement and, when passed, VIP will become an entirely paperless process.

The technology is basic, very straightforward, and easy to use. The state dedicated resources to purchase the necessary hardware and software. The challenge, therefore, was not to incorporate a proven technology, nor to raise the necessary revenues, but rather to introduce a new way of thinking to people entrenched in an old way of doing business. This included purchasing department employees as well as vendors. Employees were involved in redesigning the process from the very beginning, making recommendations on how to improve the system. It took only 10 weeks to design and implement the departmental changes because employees were excited about the changes that were to take place and took pride in the fact they were involved in a program that was on the cutting edge.

Fourteen weeks prior to going on-line, the Department of General Services initiated a statewide campaign to inform and educate potential vendors about the change that was to take place January 1. Enclosed with the bid packet was a question-and-answer brochure about VIP and a schedule of training seminars conveniently located throughout the state. Over 50,000 pieces of mail were sent directly to registered and potential vendors, letting them know the state was making it easier for them to do business by providing opportunities to bid on over $150 million worth of goods and services annually.

AUTOMATION FOR ENHANCED PRODUCTIVITY

Automation is often thought of as reducing employment. Several EXSL cases, however, demonstrate that the creative application of automated programs can help overburdened agencies make better use of their "people power," improving both their effectiveness and their benefit/cost ratios.

Computer Matching. Typically, children living with single parents in this country do not get the financial support they deserve from their noncustodial parents. Even when a court orders noncustodial parents to pay child support, only half actually comply. The state of Massachusetts recognized that regular child support payments not only raise the custodial family's standard of living but also play an important part in encouraging single parents to enter the workforce and leave welfare. The challenge for the state was to ensure that custodial families receive their court-ordered child support payments on a regular basis.

The principal enforcement tool of child support enforcement agencies like the Massachusetts Department of Revenue (DOR) is the wage assignment system: An employer deducts the support from the noncustodial parent's weekly paycheck for delivery to the custodial family. But many noncustodial parents change jobs to try to avoid their support obligation. New employers do not know they should deduct the payments from the employee's paycheck until the state informs them of the obligation. Under ordinary circumstances, however, the state will not learn of an employer's new employees until the employer submits its wage reporting data, which it does on a quarterly basis. By the time the state has reviewed quarterly wage reporting data and located the noncustodial parent at the new job, months may have elapsed. In the meantime, the noncustodial parent may have again moved on.

To foil this avoidance tactic, Massachusetts implemented the *Automated New Hire Program,* a comprehensive project requiring all employers to inform the DOR of any new employee within 14 days of hiring, although employers are encouraged to report new employees on the first day of hire by making the reporting process as quick and easy as possible:

The only information necessary is that which is already required on the W-4 form most new employees complete on their first day at work (name, address, Social Security number, and start date). A flexible filing method is used as employers may mail, fax, paper list, or electronically transfer the W-4. The DOR's computer matches this "new hire" information with records of parents who owe child support, and automatically sends out a notice to the new employer reinstating the wage assignment whenever it finds a match. If the computer finds that the employee also owes past-due support, it automatically increases the wage assignment by 25% to recover the past-due support as well. The automated new hire program allows the state to reinstate wage assignments in a matter of days, rather than the months it often took before. As a result, collections increased by $14.5 million in the program's first year of operation, and $21.6 million in welfare costs have been avoided. This cost-saving and stream-lined process is one that can be easily replicated by other jurisdictions around the country.

Computerized Ballot Box. Automation can also extend to the privacy of the voting booth. The City of Burton, Michigan, was the first locality in the United States to utilize a totally automated voting registration system: *Computer Verification of Voting Records at the Polls.* Designed to prepare the public for voting by computer (which will eventually replace manual voting and voter registration), this program involves the use of portable computers and customized software designed to verify registration data, route the voter to his or her appropriate district, and streamline the process of updating new or different voter information.

Burton experienced a great savings in terms of efficiency, accuracy, and record keeping. In terms of registration, the computerized system required approximately 5 minutes to update 2,000 names, as opposed to one day if completed manually. This translates into significant labor-cost savings, as well as increasing the accuracy with which the information is recorded. The program has enjoyed a direct and measurable impact on the residents in terms of expediting the voting process, decreasing the overall cost of elections (fewer poll workers are required), and increasing the comfort level of the voting public. One notable innovation is the process of downloading centralized voter registration data onto portable computers, which are then used at the poll site. This eliminates the need for third-party data revision and of possible duplication of effort at the polls by data entry clerks.

Not only has this program increased efficiency and reduced costs for the City of Burton but, more important, it has increased the ability for citizens to vote. No longer are citizens denied the right to vote due to administrative errors, nor are they told they must go to the clerk's office to resolve an issue because centralized voter registration data is not available at the polling site.

Computerized Jury Box. Computerization can apply to the jury box as well as the ballot box. In Athens, Georgia, the *Automated Juror Selection and Jury Tracking System* provides a computerized system that uniquely tracks juror eligibility. This system has resulted in administrative efficiency and cost savings, and is a model for smaller governments.

The program is an automated, on-line juror selection and tracking system. An innovative part of the system, apart from simply automating the selection process on a random basis, is the ability to track juror eligibility for both the state court and the superior courts. This system was designed to comply with all legal requirements and represents considerable savings in money, estimated at more than $50,000 per year. Automated selection is cost-effective and cost-efficient, and has the support and approval of state and superior court judges who view it as a vast improvement over the prior cumbersome, costly, and time-consuming manual process. The Juror Tracking subsystem tracks juror eligibility throughout the life of a given Jury Box (pool of potential jurors), including exhaustion of all jurors in the pool necessitating "Turning of the Box" (when the jurors in the box are all used or ineligible, and a new box has not been authorized, the box continues to track eligibility of all jurors, and selections continue until a new box is prepared and certified for use).

Judges are very pleased with the jury panel selection process, as are the jurors. The fact that a juror's history and eligibility status are completely and accurately tracked has enhanced the selection process. As a result, juries that are drawn are truly randomly and impartially selected and juries are free from tampering and human error. The same jurors do not need to appear repeatedly panel after panel, and jury responsibilities are shared by an impartial and representative population.

Tax-by-Telephone. The Massachusetts Department of Revenue processed 150 tons of paper tax returns every year. Paper returns are costly to process and store because they consume an incredible number of employee hours to open, sort, process, and file. The average taxpayer in Massachusetts could expect to wait 3 weeks, and citizens filing at the last minute could expect a 6-week wait, to receive a refund check.

Due to budget cuts and the mandate to "do more with less," the department had to reduce the size of its staff by 21% over a 4-year period from 1990 to 1994. Technology enabled it to accomplish that goal and provide the citizens of the state with an easier way to file their personal income tax. *Telefile,* an interactive voice response system, is one of the first electronic filing systems that requires absolutely no paper. The system accepts a voice signature rather than a signature card. There is no need to submit a W-2 form, because that data is already stored in a wage reporting database filed by employers. Taxpayers enter the system with their personal identification number (PIN), and Telefile instantaneously compares the data entered by a taxpayer against tax data from previous years to verify the identity of the taxpayer and verify the legitimacy of the income claimed.

Where the old-fashioned paper method took 3 to 6 weeks to process returns, the new paperless method is processed immediately and taxpayers can expect a refund in 4 business days. Telefile is significantly more efficient than the labor-intensive processing of paper tax returns, which cost $1.28 per return. Not only has the Department of Revenue reduced costs by 80%, but customers are better served. Telefile increases data integrity by reducing the data entry error rate virtually to zero because each data element is verified by the taxpayer as the call is made.

Since filing a tax return over the phone is very different than filing a form on paper, the biggest obstacle to address was taxpayers' behavior. The department encouraged taxpayer participation in the way it distributed forms and through an incentive, or "prize," program. To help influence the way taxpayers filed, tax returns forms were not mailed out; therefore, taxpayers who wanted to file the "old-fashioned" way had to pick up a tax return form themselves. Instead of receiving a tax return in the mail, taxpayers received booklets explaining the new and preferred way of filing. In addition, through private sector donations, the state was able to offer cash prizes to taxpayers who filed by phone, the earlier the better. As the Telefile booklet states, "You can WIN! As an additional incentive to Telefile, the program includes prize incentives. From January through mid-April, you'll get up to 20 chances to win gift certificates worth $250, $1,000 and $2,500. The earlier you file, the more chances you have to win."

This approach proved successful. During the first week, Telefile numbers surpassed the most optimistic projections with more than 17,000 filings. In its first year, 172,000 taxpayers filed their claims by the deadline using Telefile. The combined approach of "force-feeding" of the Telefile option and offering cash incentives helped change taxpayers' behavior. The user-friendly system and fast refund turnaround time is attracting more taxpayers to the Telefile system every year.

Finding Fingerprints. Technology enabled criminal justice administrators from 10 western states to form a partnership—the not-for-profit Western Identification Network (WIN)—for the development of a multistate *Automated Fingerprint Identification System (AFIS).* WIN implements and manages a cooperative system to help solve crimes, expedite the investigative process, and cut costs associated with criminal proceedings.

Under WIN, the states of Alaska, California, Idaho, Nevada, Oregon, Utah, Washington, and Wyoming successfully consolidated their funding efforts, and since its inception in 1988, WIN has grown in membership and now includes the U.S. Postal Inspections Service, U.S. Secret Service, U.S. Immigration and Naturalization Service, and the state of Montana. The program allows each of its members to conduct a fingerprint search against approximately 1.2 million records. When fingerprints are recovered from a crime scene, a fingerprint search can be launched from the respective state for a combined six-state search and, if needed, the four networked systems.

Prior to WIN, criminals could commit a crime in one state, then cross state boundaries in hopes of eluding law enforcement officers and commit the same or other crimes. It was virtually impossible and cost-prohibitive to search manually for an unidentified fingerprint against a state's manual file.

The most impressive aspect of this collaborative concept was the willingness and cooperative spirit on the part of governors, attorneys general, law enforcement administrators, and managers to agree upon a goal and overcome obstacles to achieving that goal. For example, the task of combining state-based resources for purchasing an AFIS was substantial, requiring many hours of researching state laws, preparing written documentation, requesting information, and attending AFIS workshops conducted by vendors. Equally important was the support and determination of local law enforcement officials, who were able to convince their state legislators to fund such a program. WIN's AFIS continues to be a cooperative state and federal team effort.

DELIVERING ON THE PUBLIC'S DEMANDS

The bulk of technology-based improvements in government are increments in quality. More award-winning uses of technology are primarily linked to better quality than to other factors. Although saving money is often an important corollary consideration, in some cases the public is clearly demanding clean water or improved skills, and significant investments may be necessary to accomplish those goals.

Technology for Teaching. As we approach the 21st century, education is emerging as a key element that will help us face the challenges of a rapidly changing society. Schools must be prepared to move in a new direction if those challenges are to be met. Schools need to adapt to the rapid changes and become proactive in order to lead us out of the "factory era" into the "information age." No longer will basic skills be sufficient for attaining meaningful employment. Students will need to acquire high-level, problem-solving skills to become self-directed learners, and they need to master the new tools of technology in order to be competitive.

Hunterdon Central School District in New Jersey is responding to these challenges and has made a commitment to educating students to be self-directed learners. *Schools in the Age of Technology* is a concerted effort on the part of teachers and administrators to provide the highest quality and most technologically advanced levels of education for their students.

A significant investment has been made on the part of the school district to upgrade the existing structures and install state-of-the-art technology in the schools. The goal of providing the highest-quality and most technologically advanced education has been achieved through a campuswide fiber-optic backbone; classroom computers, telephones, and video receivers; student-run television and radio stations; and state-of-the-art prototype classrooms in physics, applied technology, biochemistry, and fine arts.

The Central Board of Education decided to transform the outdated and underused wood and metal shops, a reflection of the "factory era," into applied technology and biochemistry labs, reflecting a shift to the "information age." Though these labs are nontraditional as classrooms, they are typical of the work environment students will face upon graduation. The biochemistry lab is equipped with advanced instructional technology including fully equipped lab islands, multimedia work stations, and computers networked to the library. The applied technology lab is equipped with robotics, a hands-on manipulation area, a multimedia station, and computers linked to the libraries. Not only do students benefit from these state-of-the-art labs, the faculty use the labs as staff-development centers where training for the application of technology to the classroom takes place.

The library at Hunterdon Central serves as the nerve center of the school. The library provides access to a wide spectrum of resources through technology. CD-ROMs access entire encyclopedias and bring the pages to life through graphics, sound, and animation. Access to electronic databases makes it possible to extend school beyond the classroom walls—24 hours a day. This means students and staff can do extensive research on their projects in the evening or on weekends by dialing up the school library from home. All classrooms are equipped with computers and are part of a wide area network, linked to each other and the library through fiber optics and other cable wiring. Students in a comparative world studies class, for instance, can access up-to-the-minute information from the Associated Press, geographic databases, or other graphic and text materials.

A democratized management system was used to make decisions about staff development and training, changes in schedule, and new and innovative instructional strategies. Teachers, support staff, and students collaborated fully with the administration to ensure that the needs of everyone involved were recognized. The investments in technology, and the resulting curriculum, are a reflection of the comprehensive planning that took place prior to the purchase and installation of any new equipment.

Technology for Public Assistance. Retention of a depository bank for AFDC clients was a long-term problem in Ramsey County, Minnesota, with area banks asserting that public assistance clients congested their lobbies and necessitated additional personnel during the period in which they cashed their benefits checks. To overcome this problem, Ramsey County launched the *Electronic Benefit System (EBS),* which enhanced the delivery of public assistance benefits through an existing network of automated teller machines (ATMs) located throughout the county. The system issues clients' benefits electronically, offering withdrawals through a network of ATMs. At the time of implementation there were approximately 11,000 clients receiving checks representing more than $4.5 million in monthly AFDC, Refugee Assistance, General Assistance, and Minnesota Supplemental Income Assistance. Clients are now able to access their benefits through three ATM networks, and thus do not have to worry about benefits being lost or stolen. Through customer surveys, recipients of public assistance indicate that the EBS program is more convenient than receiving a check, and they are better able to manage their money, as they do not have to withdraw all of the benefits at once. The EBS program serves 88% of the potential clientele, and there are strong indications that client support and satisfaction are high. Eligibility workers determine whether EBS is appropriate for new enrollees, and alternative delivery is arranged for people who are handicapped or do not have access to an ATM. This program eliminates the need for thousands of paper transactions, as checks are no longer issued to the majority of the county's public assistance clients. There is strong public support as well, as the EBS program is no costlier than the old method of check issuance. As other benefits, such as food stamps, are added to the electronic system, the county will realize increased program cost savings.

Curbside Bar Codes. Bar codes are commonplace in the checkout line at the grocery store. However, they are an uncommon sight along the curbs and alleys of American cities, with the exception of St. Louis Park, Minnesota. Confronted with a landfill overload problem, the city adapted "supermarket technology" to an innovative system of recycling that has significantly reduced the amount of waste sent to the overloaded landfill.

The city's objective is to reward residents who help solve landfill problems through recycling with lower garbage bills than their nonrecycling counterparts. In order to offer a financial incentive to cooperative residents, the city had to find a cost-effective way to keep track of homeowners who voluntarily recycle. Information about recycling participation had to be collected along 125 miles of city streets and alleys in all kinds of weather (such as the harsh Minnesota winter, which adversely affects the ability to gather such information). Manual data collection proved to be inefficient, inaccurate, and costly.

Integrating Bar Code Technology With Curbside Recycling resolved such problems through the use of bar code technology along curbs and alleys. When they pick up recyclables, recycling collection contractors use handheld computers to scan bar code stickers found at the curb of each individual residence. Information collected at the curb, which contains the name, location, and account number of the participating household, is later electronically fed into the city's utility billing system for more than 12,000 accounts. If the household recycles at least once a month, their quarterly refuse bill is credited by $6.60. Recycling participation—which is entirely voluntary—jumped from 45% to 90% in response to this financial incentive. In addition to the impact on the 12,047 individual garbage bills, there is communitywide impact: Less garbage is being buried in scarce landfill space. Currently the city diverts 26% of its garbage from the waste stream by recycling. The total cost to implement the bar coding program was only $30,000. The monthly cost for the previous system of manually entering participation data was $3,000; bar coding paid for itself in only 10 months.

COST-EFFECTIVE APPLICATIONS

Government's best technological practices are models for saving both time and money. Just as private citizens or the private sector seek to reduce downtime, the public sector has the same agenda, reducing unproductive travel time or waiting time.

Timesaving Telecommunications. Washington Interactive Television (WIT) is Washington state's public video telecommunications system. This statewide interactive television network allows elected officials, state agencies, municipal governments, public schools, state colleges and universities, and the average citizen to communicate in a faster, easier, less expensive, and more effective fashion. Interactive television replaces the "old fashioned" methods of communication and training that typically involved a great deal of travel time.

From Seattle to Spokane, from Vancouver to Bellingham, WIT creates a video telecommunications infrastructure that allows public employees and state citizens to save time and money otherwise spent on travel. WIT services include a broadcast-quality television studio, satellite uplink services, satellite downlink and cable channel coordination, video production, a 13-point two-way video-conferencing system, and dial-up access worldwide. This effort is bringing state-of-the-art technology to Washington in a way that is educational, innovative, and appropriate for the state and its citizens. Experts from around the state, nation, and the world have been part of satellite broadcasts via a two-way video-conferencing interface.

WIT is built on the success of several years of demonstration projects and partnerships. Interfacing satellite technology with a terrestrial compressed digital video-conference system has created a video infrastructure with maximum capabilities, facilitating communication, flexibility, and access.

The value of WIT as a means of saving time and money, increasing access to government, and fostering better statewide communication includes instances in which

- The Governor holds a public hearing on education reform with citizens in rural communities who otherwise would not have had the opportunity to speak out and be heard.
- The director of the Department of Wildlife "meets" with approximately 800 employees across the state on a quarterly basis, enabling staff to have direct access to top management and increased communication.
- Citizens in Spokane testify before commissioners of the Washington Utilities and Transportation Commission in Olympia 250 miles away, a distance that would have prevented most citizens from participating and providing comment on an important issue.
- State representatives conduct video "town meetings" during the legislative session on issues important to constituents at home.
- High-quality yet inexpensive video production enables agencies to provide professional training programs for employees, reduce travel costs, and create flexible training sessions.

Facilitating Applications. Citizens often experienced long delays when applying to the City of Phoenix Neighborhood Improvement and Housing Department (NIH). To overcome this problem, the agency established an *Intergovernmental Computer Link-Up* to better facilitate the application process by reducing duplication of effort, minimizing delays, and reducing the paper-intensive clerical costs to the city.

The Link-Up, an integrated computer system, has increased efficiency. The agency worked to link up formerly incompatible computer systems, and the information transfer process between the two systems was redesigned so that the clerical staff could easily access both systems from the same terminal. Phoenix's NIH was the first non-law enforcement agency to be tied into the state's computer system, something that enabled the city to determine eligibility for applicants' income and family composition almost immediately. It reduced delays by at least 2 weeks, eliminated a second applicant interview, and more accurately calculated rental subsidies for families receiving public assistance. As the program became more successful, the system was redesigned to accommodate additional information and now serves as a clearinghouse for all Arizona housing authorities.

Link-Up ensures that public housing tenants are income eligible, which eventually results in fewer evictions and administrative costs. Incorporating this technology has resulted in an annualized cost avoidance of more than $500,000, and an annualized revenue increase of more than $25,000. Link-Up ensures that the most qualified, eligible applicants are selected for a limited number of housing units, keeping these as crime- and drug free as possible. An initial investment of $13,000 covered the cost of hardware and software and a small amount of programming.

CROSS-CUTTING TECHNIQUES

Some jurisdictions do more than just seek out and adapt technologies. They develop and apply comprehensive approaches to the management of tangible assets, incorporating both low-tech and high-tech approaches.

Responding Rapidly. New York City's capital construction process is often too protracted and too costly. As a time-efficient and cost-effective alternative to this process, the city's Bureau of Facilities Management (BFM) developed the *Facilities Action Strategy Team (FAST),* an in-house design and construction team with the mission of responding rapidly to facilities' problems. Prior to establishing an in-house team, the city used outside contractors that were costly and often the cause of many unnecessary delays. FAST is a 26-member unit, composed of architects, engineers, and tradesmen, many with private sector experience. FAST addresses the problem of efficiently completing the construction and conversion of space to meet the city's changing needs. Without FAST, the process of constructing critical facilities would be significantly longer.

In a city such as New York, emergencies and unforeseen circumstances require a rapid response on the part of the Bureau of Facilities Management. However, the use of outside contractors and the existing bureaucratic structure made it exceedingly difficult for the BFM to respond in a timely and cost-effective manner. A case in point is the city's procurement process. Designed to guarantee equal access for eligible vendors, the process is often time-consuming and cumbersome. An entire construction project can be delayed waiting for a vendor to deliver sheetrock or by the inordinate amount of lead time necessary to comply with purchasing procedures.

FAST redesigned the standard city purchasing procedures, allowing modified blanket orders and requirement contracts to be used. This change provided the BFM with continual purchasing capabilities and allowed contractors to bid on a variety of construction materials at one time. Under this new format, one vendor could provide a variety of miscellaneous products for electrical work, painting, hardware, and suspended ceiling components.

Without appropriate facilities in which to operate innovative programs, innovations fail. For example, New York City designed an innovative program to streamline the arrest-arraignment process within the judicial system. The new program required additional holding pens and client interview booths, problems of physical capacity that FAST addressed.

Utilizing FAST has allowed the city to save money, increase the quality of construction, and ultimately improve city services in a wide variety of projects in which facilities' problems must be solved immediately. FAST projects resulted in time savings of between 50% and 67% and cost savings of between 20% and 50%, depending upon the project.

Sharing Innovations. New York City is prone not only to the procedural gridlock that FAST addresses, but to problems in sharing useful information among managers. Limited communication within and among more than 40 separate agencies, each with its own independent computer bureau and multiple computer systems, inhibits exchange of information and mutual problem solving. Communications within and among agencies can be difficult.

Identification and funding of useful computer-based projects led to formation of the *Micro-Minicomputer Coordinating Council (M2C2),* an organization of computer managers. With the M2C2 organization, agencies can network ideas and share solutions to problems. For example, the Citywide Productivity Forum, sponsored by M2C2, is now a major event for the computer community within city government. The forum honors and recognizes computer technicians, who are seldom acknowledged for their contributions; it allows for the exchange of ideas through its publication of agencies' projects; and it has led to increased morale and productivity within the computer community, all of which has led to improved public service. Award-winning initiatives highlight cost savings and operations improvements totaling millions of dollars. Most projects are easily transferable to other agencies. ,

The productivity forum also provides the following:

1. Opportunities for an exchange of ideas and applications in increasing productivity.
2. A Technology Investment Fund, conceived by M2C2 as a special account created by The Fund for the City of New York that is used to finance promising, small-scale technology-based projects. The forum's publication raises money for the Technology Investment Fund through paid advertising from private sector computer firms.

Other than publication printing costs, the forum costs the city nothing while raising revenues for the fund.

Coordinating Construction. The City of Houston needed to control waste-water overflows as mandated by the federal government (EPA) and the Texas Natural Resources Conservation Commission. In response, the *Greater Houston Wastewater Program (GHWP)*, a Division of the city's Department of Public Works and Engineering, planned expenditures of over $1 billion over 3 years, most of it in sewer rehabilitation and new relief sewers. The construction work, affecting a large part of the 5,600-mile sewer collection system and covering almost the whole city, was on an unprecedented scale.

To minimize the construction impact of this work and to avoid conflicts with other agencies, an Interagency Coordination Committee was formed by the GHWP in early 1993. The committee is composed of representatives from the various city, county, and state agencies involved in construction activity within the Greater Houston area, including GHWP, city road and water departments, Harris County Engineer's Department, Harris County Flood Control District, Metro, and the Texas Department of Transportation (TxDOT). The committee meets on a regular basis, collating all available data on current and future projects within their respective capital improvement programs.

It became apparent that the large number of projects involved would require the use of a Geographical Information System (GIS). Intergraph equipment and software were selected for the graphical display and database of all the projects. Layering allows the plotting of each agency's projects on a map or digital orthophoto base for visual checking. Color coding of the projects permits immediate identification of the relevant agency or division responsible. To date, some 3,300 projects representing 10 agencies or divisions of agencies have been identified and incorporated into the records.

The results achieved from this initiative have demonstrated the cost benefit of the coordination effort, not only to the Greater Houston Wastewater Program but also to the other agencies. Communication among agencies has improved, conflicts have been identified, and resolution of problems has been reached. Initial skepticism changed into unreserved enthusiasm.

The program addresses two issues: the costs associated with additional construction and contractor delay claims, and citizens' dissatisfaction, either of which may result from construction conflicts that could occur through a failure of agencies to plan ahead. *Conflict* is defined in different ways according to the specific case. Simultaneous construction by two agencies on a certain street is an obvious example. Another example would be a resurfaced road being affected by trench excavation within 2 years of completion of the paving work. Prolonged disruption to a neighborhood or to businesses through sequential work (which might restrict traffic flow or adversely affect the public patronage of businesses for an unreasonable amount of time) would also qualify as a conflict.

The total cost to the Greater Houston Wastewater Program for the interagency coordination effort to date is approximately $305,000, inclusive of labor and nonlabor expenditures. This represents the cost of setting up the system, collecting data from all the participating agencies, and preparing the first volume of color graphics for each agency, together with a database listing of more than 3,300 projects. It is a living document that requires regular and routine updating. The cost to GHWP of providing this ongoing service is expected to be between $30,000 and $40,000 a month against projects totaling approximately $1.1 billion. Construction began in 1994 and will end in December 1997, with an average expenditure of $23 million per month. That is, only 0.17% of the construction cost is being spent to avoid conflicts. The benefits of enhanced coordination through the use of technology clearly outweigh the costs.

CONCLUSION

Adopting new technologies can be as simple as using a fax machine to provide up-to-date information on the employment status of noncustodial parents, as creative as using existing bar code technology to monitor recycling compliance, or as complex as setting up an interstate fingerprint identification system to track offenders. Public employees have no shortage of such ideas, and they freely "put them on the table" when asked. But in comparison to the private sector, they do suffer from a shortage of capital to invest in productive innovations.

The public sector could apply many more productive, cost-saving, quality-enhancing technological innovations if funding were available. The innovations above were accomplished with minimal funding by private sector standards, but they were successful despite the "handicaps" by which public agencies are typically limited:

- the political nature of the budget process
- multiyear delays in approving requests for capital investments
- prohibitions on reinvesting savings in their own agencies

If government is to be more "businesslike," then the private sector has to support its public counterparts in raising funds for comparable investments in technology: state-of-the-art computers, comfortable buildings, timely information systems, and so on. Despite the technological creativity that EXSL and other award programs evidence—*Government Technology* (1987-1997) for example, highlights scores of technological applications in the public sector on a monthly basis—it is unrealistic to expect many governments to be able to squeeze expensive investments from budgets that are declining in real dollars. That is, government must be allowed to overcome a blatant double standard in which the private sector is expected to make capital investments necessary to do its jobs, but the public sector is starved for the capital investments that would help support the public infrastructure that businesses need to be profitable: for example, transportation to work and market, public schools for a developing workforce, water and sewers for a developing economy.

REFERENCES

Government Technology: Solutions for State and Local Government in the Information Age. (1987-1997). Vols. I-X.
NASA (National Aeronautic and Space Administration), Office of Technology Applications. (1996). Washington, D.C. 1997.
Public Employees Roundtable. (various years). *List of government inventions.* Washington, DC: Author.

5

BUILDING
PARTNERSHIPS

■

Building Partnerships

Community Partnerships—Citizens and Volunteers ─
Public Sector Partners ─
Private Sector Partners ─
Not-for-Profit Partners ─┘

PARTNERSHIPS, NOT PRIVATIZATION
■

Despite "businesslike" innovations in quality, human resources, and technology, the rush to privatize government has seemingly gained unstoppable momentum. Touted regularly by politicians and emphasized by the media, it is now virtually an unquestioned assumption.

The logic of privatization proponents is that turning services over to the private sector—through contracts or through abandonment—produces large savings with virtually no loss of quality or reduction in service levels (Savas, 1992). Proponents of privatization "have lived by the mantra that anything government can do, business can do better" (Katz, 1991, p. 38). Advocates hold that outsourcing can deliver a much greater portion of services that are now public. Privatization is marketed as a solution that will

■ lower costs, while improving quality
■ allow economics of scale
■ allow public versus private comparisons of cost and performance
■ avoid large start-up costs
■ provide access to specialized skills and training
■ promote flexibility in the size and mix of services
■ make it possible to hire and fire as necessary
■ allow for experimentation in different modes of service provision
■ reduce dependence on a single supplier
■ bypass inert bureaucracies
■ allow quicker response to new service areas (see Savas, 1987)

But skeptics hold that many services are necessarily government's responsibility, and a public-to-private shift will not automatically enhance productivity in a jurisdiction or department (Barnekov & Raffel, 1992). Barnekov and Raffel and other critics (see Ogilvy, 1986-1987, p. 15; Stahl, 1988, p. 42) suggest questions the public manager needs to answer when considering whether to privatize in order to enhance productivity. To what extent is privatization likely to

■ interfere with accountability?
■ degrade responsiveness?
■ reduce services?
■ lower employee morale?
■ result in incomplete contracts?
■ produce cost overruns?
■ lower quality at the expense of quantity?
■ place short-term profits over long-term planning?
■ negate the service ideal inherent in public service?
■ provide opportunities for graft and corruption?
■ duplicate services?

A recurring theme in the privatization literature is that what makes a difference is competition between the sectors, not privatization itself, and that private monopolies are no better than the public ones (Donahue, 1984). According to Savas (1987), cost-saving competition will, for instance, encourage innovation by allowing for experimentation in different modes of service provision, bypassing inert bureaucracies and allowing quicker response to new service areas.

Privatization is thus only one form of competition, a form limited to the private sector; an equally productive alternative is an expanded form of competition in which public organizations are competitive bidders. Some cities, such as Phoenix and Indianapolis (see Chapter 2), have pioneered public-private competition, and in head-to-head competition with private bidders have often won those bids.

Increasing Competition. In Phoenix, the Department of Public Works established a program that utilizes a nontraditional approach to competing with private industry in order to increase productivity and significantly cut agency costs.

Faced with growing budget problems, Phoenix was increasingly awarding municipal contracts to private organizations. In response, the Department of Public Works created *Competition With Privatization* to enhance the competitive atmosphere in which it operates through increased technology, labor-management cooperation, innovative practices, and community involvement and support. The focus of the program is on solid waste collection, which impacts every household and provides citizens a means to evaluate municipal services on a firsthand basis. In 1995, savings and cost-avoidance totaled approximately $3.3 million dollars.

The program has also engendered improved employee moral and labor-management relations, which has resulted in productivity enhancements, innovations (e.g., retread tires), and participation in the competitive bidding process by department employees, as well as cooperation between unions and the city. At present, the City of Phoenix has earned back all contracts that were previously lost to private contractors.

While competition is certainly an important assumption, it is not the only paradigm. The "flip side" of competition—cooperation—is also an essential productivity enhancement strategy, and one that is very often overlooked in the shadow of pressures for privatization. Yet joint public-private initiatives are options to which innovative public officials often turn, and cooperative arrangements for service provision are increasingly evident as the public sector seeks creative ways to stretch resources.

In contrast to privatization, these new relationships are joint problem-solving efforts, or partnerships, that may be initiated by either "side." EXSL has recognized working alliances between the workforce and management; between levels of government and between neighboring local governments; and between government and citizens, government and corporations, government and not-for-profits. These innovations have proven to be effective arrangements aimed at improving government service and cutting costs. Because they represent the ability to think and act outside the rigid but familiar "bureaucratic box," they can be essential for pooling resources and improving productivity in an increasingly resource-scarce atmosphere.

EXSL cases highlight different forms of partnerships that enhance productivity improvements in public organizations. Award-winning programs often occur in one of four types of partnerships with

- Communities and volunteers
- Public agencies
- Private corporations
- Not-for-profits

COMMUNITY PARTNERSHIPS—
■ CITIZENS AND VOLUNTEERS

Government's partners are most often the citizens it serves. Sometimes they coproduce services because they are required to by law: maintaining a sidewalk, carrying garbage to the curb, driving children to school. But, if afforded the opportunity, citizens are often eager to contribute their time and creative energies and to cooperate with service agencies.

Community Partnerships. The Public Library plays an integral role in the city of San Diego's *Neighborhood Pride and Protection Program (NPP)*. The program is dedicated to enhancing the quality of life for all San Diegans by forming community partnerships within neighborhoods to broaden the scope and impact of city services.

Many of the San Diego communities, particularly the densely populated, ethnically diverse inner-city communities, have experienced a deteriorating quality of life in which young people are particularly vulnerable. NPP addresses the underlying problems associated with at-risk youth ages 4 through 18. These problems include an insufficiency of the following:

- Educational skills that could help improve self-esteem
- Safe places for children and young adults to gather

- Organized efforts to reinforce school curricula
- Facilities and programs that provide opportunities for family involvement

Addressing these needs, NPP has improved the delivery of library services through three major elements: expanded library hours, the establishment of Homework Centers, and the provision of Youth Services Librarians. Expanded hours at 3 area libraries, 12 branch libraries, and the central library, which keep the libraries open later in the evenings and on Sundays, have served to provide an opportunity for additional use of library facilities for recreational reading, to study and to complete homework assignments, or to seek tutorial assistance. The Homework Centers offer a productive environment, particularly after school hours. The addition of full-time youth services librarians at central and branch libraries enhances outreach and cooperative efforts with local schools and community agencies, and provides special interest programming to attract youth to the library.

One of the main purposes of NPP is to form community partnerships and interdepartmental cooperation. At most Homework Centers, two or three volunteers aid students with homework and literacy skills. Satellite Centers are located in City of San Diego Park and Recreation facilities as well as in neighborhood-based agencies such as Boys' Clubs and Girls' Clubs, YMCAs, and homeless shelters. In the past 2 years, more than $30,000 has been donated by private sources to establish and maintain Homework Centers. Over $282,000 in state and federal funds have been awarded for specific target groups such as new immigrants (Asian and Hispanic), youth, senior, and limited English-speaking populations, and family literacy. Over 75% of these funds have been earmarked for NPP programs. The library has allocated $4,810,855 of its general funds over the past 3 years to establish and support NPP. The success of the centers is measured by computer use, tutor/student matches, the condition of the collections and equipment, youth circulation, and door count; a survey evaluating output measures is planned. Extended Sunday service now accounts for 5% of the total circulation system wide. Students are the largest user group, based on informal staff input. In fiscal year (FY) 93, over 75,000 children attended programs, including summer programs. From July 1993 to January 1994, more than 49,593 children attended programs at central and branch libraries. Nine new youth services librarians, hired and trained to serve San Diego communities, have successfully attracted more children to participate in programs. There has been a corresponding increase in usage of Homework Center computers. In FY 95, almost 50,000 children used these computers.

Community Policing. The Alexandria, Virginia, Police Department introduced the *Residential Police Officer (RPO)* program in the fall of 1992 as a pilot program aimed at reducing serious crime in one of the city's most vulnerable neighborhoods. In the RPO program, a veteran police officer moves into a selected public housing community or other low-income neighborhood, which becomes the residential police officer's patrol "beat."

The RPO program represents a marked departure from traditional police work, which consists of patrol officers responding to calls for service as directed by a police dispatcher. Traditionally, the police officer's responsibility has been very narrowly defined: respond to crime scenes, take a report, make arrests, assist crime victims, and respond to the dispatcher's next call. Police officers have little time to engage in community organizing activities that in the long run enable neighborhoods to promote the health, welfare, and safety of their residents and help them to resist crime. In addition to patrolling the neighborhood on foot, the residential police officer is on duty 24 hours a day and is responsible for enlisting neighborhood residents in an organized effort to reduce crime and solve other community problems.

All three residential police officers are veteran officers who volunteered for the assignment and received special training in community problem solving. They reside in public housing units provided by the Alexandria Redevelopment and Housing Authority and their "beat" assignment is to provide police services 24 hours a day to their neighborhood. They are also responsible for recruiting community leaders and involving residents in the development and implementation of solutions to community problems identified by the residents themselves. Community acceptance of the program is high. The resident police officers are well-respected members of their new neighborhoods. Serious crime (homicide, rape, robbery, assault, burglary, larceny) has decreased by as much as 35% in the RPO districts.

Supplementing Police. The *Mayor's Handicap Parking Enforcement Team (HPET)* of Flint, Michigan, was established to help meet the educational and enforcement concerns of handicap parking issues. As a result of budget constraints due to a high unemployment rate, declining population, and decreasing revenue, the Flint Police Department has experienced a dramatic reduction in the number of its officers on the street. This, plus a high rate of crime, often necessitated making the enforcement of handicap parking laws a low priority within the department. To help remedy this problem, volunteers were trained and authorized to issue tickets to violators of handicap parking laws. Four dozen HPET volunteers, working cooperatively with the Police Department, the secretary of state's office, and Department of Building Inspections, address four major problem areas concerning handicap parking: (a) enforcement, (b) the addition of correctly signed spaces, (c) public relations, and (d) distribution of handicap parking permit information. There has been a dramatic improvement in the availability of handicap parking spaces in Flint, and 400 additional spaces have been placed at local businesses by UAW Job Bank volunteers. Through funding received from the City Council, donations, fund-raisers, and ticket revenue the project is completely self-supporting.

PUBLIC SECTOR PARTNERS

Government agencies often serve the clients of other agencies. Cooperation between those agencies is important in minimizing costs, especially when the "products" of one agency become the "workload" of another.

Reducing Costs. The *Medicaid Metropass Program,* a joint venture by the state of Florida Agency for Health Care Administration and the Metro Dade County Transit Agency, was designed to provide unlimited public transportation to selected Medicaid recipients who forgo the use of their individualized Medicaid transportation to medical appointments. Medicaid recipients who were using individualized Medicaid transport a minimum of six times per month were invited to participate in this program. After an initial successful 6 months of operation, the program was expanded to include individuals from 12 different community agencies (e.g., mental health centers, AIDS support networks, and senior citizen centers) that served Medicaid clients who have frequent need for transportation to Medicaid-compensable services.

Cost savings are calculated monthly using a formula based on actual transportation charges incurred for the previous 3 months or based on community agency projections of scheduled appointments for the current month. The number of trips per month by people included in this program has ranged from a minimum of 6 to a maximum of 46 (for a client who attends a mental health day treatment program 5 times a week and also has medical appointments scheduled during the month). The cost of a one-way para-transit trip is $15.73; the cost of a monthly discounted transit pass is $31.63. Savings per client range from a minimum of $94.38 per month to a maximum of $723.58 each month.

The Metropass program created a win-win situation: for the Florida taxpayers, a dramatic documented cost savings; for Medicaid clients, increased mobility and independence; for Metro Dade County, increased public transportation ridership and therefore increased revenue; and for private providers, more dependable transportation for their clients.

Developing Business. During the 1980s, Montgomery County, Ohio, faced economic pressures and fiscal constraints similar to those that plagued other local governments during that period: rising public service costs, lower-than-forecast tax revenues, federal and state aid reductions, and a "mobile" industrial base. To cope with these trends, the county developed the *Economic Development/Government Equity (ED/GE)* program. The program seeks to strengthen the regional economic base, promote rational countywide growth, leverage other public and private development funds, and foster interlocal government cooperation. ED/GE provides $5,000,000 yearly to fund countywide economic development projects; in return, local jurisdictions that participate in the program must share a portion of their new economic growth with other communities in the county. Other development funds were leveraged by ED/GE funds by a ratio of 2:1, thousands of jobs within the county were created or retained in area businesses, and all participating jurisdictions shared in the costs and benefits of economic development.

Particularly worrisome to county officials was the number of "smoke-stack" industries undergoing retrenchment and contraction. Also of concern was the urban blight that was beginning to affect Dayton, an aging city that is home to a significant portion of the county's population. In response to these challenges and past economic trends, Montgomery County developed ED/GE to coordinate areawide economic development efforts, to reduce the costs of public goods and services, to decrease interjurisdictional competition for business, and to increase overall interlocal cooperation.

The impact of the ED/GE program is twofold. First, ED/GE seeks to spread the costs and benefits of economic development across a countywide region. This is greatly beneficial for local jurisdictions with limited fiscal means, because their development costs are not as burdensome as if they were borne alone. Essentially, they spur necessary development at a lower cost; a stronger tax base raises more tax revenues and enables poorer communities to fund essential public goods and services.

Second, ED/GE promotes interjurisdictional cooperation and partnerships. By encouraging local jurisdictions to work together on development projects and service provision, policymakers expect that the oftentimes debilitating interjurisdictional competition for businesses will lessen and local tax bases will become more stable overall. Also, more interjurisdictional cooperation can decrease the amount of duplicative development projects and can explore regional solutions to service delivery problems. Indeed, one of the studies funded through ED/GE examined the feasibility of merging many local fire and EMS services into a single district. Substantial savings can be realized for participating jurisdictions when training, maintenance, dispatch, and other essential functions are centralized.

Cooperating Across Borders. The Police of the Port Authority of New York and New Jersey, with the assistance of Bergen County (New Jersey) and New York City police officers, conduct surveillance of suspected drug buyers as they make purchases in the Washington Heights section of New York City. Under *Operation Border Crossing* the buyers are followed, and those heading to New Jersey, via the George Washington Bridge, are arrested.

The basic premises of the operation include detectives surveilling known "drug buy" locations in Washington Heights that are frequented by New Jersey- and Pennsylvania-registered vehicles for the purpose of buying illegal drugs. Following observation by Port Authority detectives of a drug buy, the vehicle and occupants are monitored during their return trip back to New Jersey, via the George Washington Bridge. Once back in New Jersey, a marked police vehicle with uniformed officers will make a vehicle stop. The stop will be based upon probable cause information supplied by detectives to the marked units. The occupants of the target vehicle will be placed under arrest for possession of narcotics. The involvement of an assistant prosecutor and members of the Bergen County Prosecutor's Office ensures conformity with established operational rules and stop, search, and seizure legal requirements.

Partnering on Probation. The *Move to Independence Program* is a unique partnership between the Probation Department and the County Office of Education in Pomona, California, that pairs juvenile delinquents with mentally and physically impaired children who need to develop basic skills. The students at the El Camino School for the Handicapped, who range in age from 3 to 22 years, have multiple physical and mental disabilities. The incarcerated juvenile offenders, who are serving sentences at the Probation Department's Camp Afflerbaugh in La Verne, California, spend 6½ hours per day, 4 days a week, helping the handicapped children to master basic skills such as eating, moving with the assistance of special equipment, sitting, strengthening muscles, standing alone, and learning to walk for the first time in their lives. One-on-one loving is stressed as being the major focus for success. Juvenile offenders volunteer for the program by submitting written applications stating what they know about the program, why they wish to participate, and what experiences and skills they bring to the program. The applications are carefully screened by both camp and school staff, as is the applicant's background and behavior while in camp as well as his or her motivation for applying for this program.

Selected applicants attend the County Schools-Work Experience program, which provides classroom instruction in job readiness skills along with specialized on-the-job training. Upon completion of the program, participants receive certificates of completion and letters of recommendation for employment. Entry level Special Education Teacher Assistant positions are available with no more than a high school diploma or GED, as are future career paths in the health care and special education fields. Since the inception of the program, handicapped students who have received the personalized care have achieved a 141% average improvement in functional motor skills, the juvenile offenders have developed compassion and marketable skills in health care and education, and the program has been replicated for girls in another county probation camp and a nearby school for handicapped students.

Technical Teaming. In early 1986, the Tidewater area of Virginia experienced a series of trench collapses that resulted in the deaths of several workers and the endangerment of numerous fire and rescue personnel. The *Tidewater Regional Technical Rescue Team* was established to organize specialized rescue services.

Each jurisdiction in the Tidewater area of Virginia provides personnel to be trained by the Virginia Beach Fire Department and then assigns those personnel to the rescue team. Funding was raised by contacting and soliciting the utility and building contractors' professional groups. The City of Virginia Beach Fire Department agreed to act as the receiving and insuring agency for all equipment and apparatus donated. As a result of this unique effort, the Tidewater area of Virginia now has 365-day-a-year provision of technical rescue services, covering five cities and all of the military installations in a 2,000-square-mile area. A total of $350,000 for equipment was raised through donations, and manpower costs are absorbed by the localities with no additional personnel costs associated with the implementation of this project. This team was selected by the Federal Emergency Management Agency (FEMA) as one of the nation's 25 task forces that will be used to respond to catastrophic disasters nationally. The program provides a service that no municipality or military installation would be able to afford to provide on its own. From a financial standpoint, it has provided each municipality with these services at a minimal cost. Since currently available manpower was used, there is no additional impact with regard to salaries or benefits.

Suppressing Sexual Abuse. The *Baltimore County Child Advocacy Center* is a highly specialized and interdisciplinary organization of four public agencies, charged with the mission of investigation, assessment, and prosecution of child sexual abuse cases. The agencies involved include the Baltimore County Department of Social Services, the Baltimore County Police Department, the Baltimore County Health Department, and the Baltimore County State's Attorney's Office. These organizations constitute the advocacy center.

In 1989, a federal grant awarded to the Baltimore County Department of Social Services permitted the organization of the County Child Advocacy Center, which facilitates investigations into cases of alleged child sexual abuse. Children who are brought to the center are seen by a pediatrician and a pediatric nurse-practitioner who specialize in child sexual abuse examinations. As the child receives expert medical care, the attending physician provides pertinent information to law enforcement and social welfare personnel who will launch their investigation of the offense. The social welfare and criminal investigations determine whether the child should be removed from the home, and assess the level of trauma to both the child and the family. Often, the center arranges for treatment and counseling to begin for the offender as well as the child. The advocacy center investigates about 600 cases of suspected child sexual abuse annually and has developed a sophisticated and sensitive method of interviewing children, one third of whom are under the age of 5. The center estimates that in 65% of their investigations, there are no findings of abuse. In cases where abuse has occurred, however, the investigative teams have proven highly successful in obtaining confessions from incest offenders. This has a positive effect on the community at large, as increased numbers of offenders undergo treatment, face incarceration, or both. The program is considered highly innovative due to its integrated approach to managing the cases of sexually abused children. Through the cooperation of four Baltimore County agencies, the child and the family are subject to a less stressful experience and are not overwhelmed by the enormity of the overall child welfare system. With coordinated effort and county support, the Baltimore Child Advocacy Center is a noteworthy model for other local governments.

Shopping for Services. Implemented in 1988 under Governor Thomas Kean, the *New Jersey School Based Youth Services Program (SBYSP)* provides comprehensive services on a one-stop-shopping basis in or near secondary schools. Sites provide the following core services: health care, mental health and family counseling, employment training, and substance abuse counseling.

The SBYSP helped to eliminate artificial boundaries between schools and various human service, health, and employment systems by creating a link among service providers that fosters a comprehensive system of care for at-risk youth. The program addresses numerous problems facing adolescents, children, and families. These problems often result in young people dropping out or not attending school, committing self-destructive acts including becoming pregnant, becoming involved with the juvenile justice system, and giving a poor academic performance. In addition, many services that are provided to this population are inaccessible and geographically dispersed throughout counties. Therefore, young people, even if they could get to the services, are often unable to. Also, the systems that young people are involved with do not interact with one another in a way that serves their clients. The SBYSP provides services at the site where the young people are most likely to be—school—and also links for the first time the various community programs and systems, including education, human services, health, and employment.

By providing services at the place where the majority of young people are found, the SBYSP is able to bring services directly to the client. Making the services convenient and client-centered has provided access and increased the use of services by young people. Also, having these agencies work together on the various problems that young people face allows the sum of the parts to become greater than the whole. The fact that more than 20,000 students and their families use these services in the core service areas is testimony to the improvement of the delivery system. In addition, the program uses recreation as an umbrella for services, creating a nonstigmatizing atmosphere. This atmosphere draws students to the program and to the caring adults who are on staff to assist young people.

This program is not measured in terms of direct cost reduction. It is measured in terms of young people attending school, improving their academic performance, not dropping out of school, and in changing their behavior to avoid ending up in one of the state's tertiary systems, such as juvenile justice or mental health institutions.

The major results of this program are that children and families receive services in a holistic way and that the systems that affect these individuals work together for the customer. In addition, this program was the springboard for developing a subcabinet interagency group of eight state departments called FamilyNet. FamilyNet was designed to foster collaboration at the state level, to remove barriers to providing services, and to work with local school districts. Finally, the last result is the thousands of young people who are now on the road to becoming productive citizens and meeting their full potential.

Integrating Service Delivery. The *General Relief Interagency Project (GRIP)* is an integrated service delivery system for general relief (GR) clients in Ventura County, California. The intent of the program is to reduce the length of time an individual stays on GR, gain reimbursement of costs by assisting clients with the social security process, reduce fragmentation of service deliveries, and increase efficiencies.

California state law mandates that counties provide for indigent persons who do not qualify for other types of aid. The General Relief (GR) program, which is totally county-funded, meets this mandate and is operated by Ventura County's Public Social Services Agency (PSSA). GR costs were increasing dramatically year after year, as the general economic climate continued to deteriorate.

The GRIP program coordinates a variety of services needed by general relief recipients to assist them to leave the program as quickly as possible. Services include job placement; job searching techniques; initiation, coordination, and monitoring of program development agreements with appropriate social services agencies; necessary case management services for employable and unemployable GR recipients; and advocacy and intervention with Social Security to assure that GR recipients who qualify for SSI apply and to expedite the SSI applications; and ensuring that the county obtains repayment from the initial SSI retroactive check.

The philosophy of the program is to provide services to clients for their long-term benefit. In addition to the services rendered, the program attempts to project an attitude that the recipients need to be held accountable for their actions and to be responsible for themselves to the extent that they are able.

General relief was providing food and shelter, but there were other needs that were not being met. Many of the clients were not able to become employed because of mental problems or limitations; drug or alcohol dependency, or both; homelessness; and physical disabilities. If they were able to work, they lacked the necessary skills to secure and maintain employment. There was also a large number of clients who were totally disabled but unable to complete the social security application progress.

The successful strategies of the GRIP program have resulted in continuous caseload and expenditure decreases. Expenditures through March 1994 were $760,200, compared to expenditures of $1,407,500 for the same period in 1991-1992—a reduction of $647,4000. In addition, the county increased SSI repayments by $342,000.

Managing Care. The *Hillsborough County [Florida] Health Care Plan* is a response to the problem of provision of health care to an indigent population with income at or below the federal poverty level. This managed care network has improved the integration of existing medical, mental health, and social services.

The Hillsborough County Health Care Plan is a response to the problem of providing of health care to an indigent population with income at or below the federal poverty level. Hillsborough County's medically indigent population had very little access to medical care and usually sought treatment through the emergency room after the onset of illness, instead of receiving primary or preventive care. The county found that the cost was exorbitant, due to uncompensated care at the only public hospital.

Hillsborough Health Care has increased access to quality health care; improved the integration of medical, mental health, and social services; enhanced prevention and education; and reduced per-patient expenditures. The number of primary care sites has increased from 4 to 16, and the number of patients served annually has risen from 15,000 to 24,000. With no premiums, copayments, deductibles, preexisting condition exclusions, or maximums, and with the inclusion of dental and vision care, the average cost per member is $294 a month. The service has diverted 11,456 potential emergency room visits at an estimated cost avoidance of more than $5,700,000 in 2 years. This managed care network includes both public and private providers and is divided into four geographic networks.

Cooperating and Coordinating. The *Criminal Justice Commission (CJC)* of Palm Beach County, Florida, is an innovative method for assisting county Commissioners to obtain better cooperation and coordination of efforts by the various criminal justice system components. In Florida, county government is responsible for a large proportion of criminal justice costs but has little authority in determining these costs. Each agency head in the criminal justice system is independently elected (e.g., the sheriff, the chief judge, the clerk of the court, state attorney, and public defender). Therefore, they are not directly accountable to the funding source, the Board of County Commissioners. To further the problem, the criminal justice system is adversarial, by nature, and too frequently this "prosecution versus defense" mentality, appropriate on a case-by-case basis in the courtroom, is carried over to administering offices. This creates extensive turf guarding and duplication of effort and costs to the county government. The only effective way to control costs is through a more cooperative criminal justice system.

The mission of the CJC is to study all aspects of the criminal justice and crime prevention systems throughout the federal, state, county, municipal, and private agencies within Palm Beach County and to make recommendations to the Board of County Commissioners on policies and programs. It is designed to accomplish an overall coordination of law enforcement and crime prevention efforts; to develop an efficient, cost-effective, and timely criminal justice system; and to assist in the reduction of crime. It is composed of 21 representatives of the public sector and 12 members of the private sector.

The CJC task forces, committees, and councils, representing over 200 representatives of criminal justice agencies and concerned citizens of Palm Beach County, identify priorities, assess alternatives, and recommend solutions to local problems. A major accomplishment of the CJC has been having key policymakers work together to improve the criminal justice system in Palm Beach County. In turn, this cooperation has accomplished numerous improvements, including the following:

- Establishing a drug court with a full treatment continuum for both criminal offenders and civil clients
- Creating a Law Enforcement Planning Council representing 37 municipalities with 31 chiefs of police
- Developing mutual aid agreements, uniform policy and procedures, and simplified DUI processing
- Disposing cooperatively of confiscated drugs
- Targeting specific vicinities through multiagency (city, county, state, federal) violent crime units in order to eliminate drive-by shootings and other violent drug-related and gang activity
- Developing an integrated CJIS (computerized Criminal Justice Information Service) including the courts, prosecutors, defense attorneys, probation departments, the clerk of court, and law enforcement

PRIVATE SECTOR PARTNERS

Joint public-private ventures may strengthen government's capacity to deliver services by

- providing donations of personnel or equipment,
- supplementing such services as schools, parks, and libraries;
- jointly developing strategies to ameliorate emerging problems, such as homelessness or crime; and
- stimulating economic development.

Private partners will generally expect their investment, typically donations of personnel and equipment, to provide at least some indirect return, such as a better-educated labor force, a safer neighborhood in which to do business, or a stimulus to economic development. But the private partner may also begin to act as a public-serving institution, directly investing for the general public good rather than for any specific, short-term bottom-line gain.

Building Affordable Housing. The state of Hawaii's Housing Finance and Development Corporation (HFDC) formed partnerships with private industry developers to create three socioeconomically integrated quality lifestyle communities in Hawaii's three highest population growth areas. These *Master Planned Communities (MPCs)* integrate a mix of for-sale single-family and multifamily homes, rental housing, neighborhood parks, schools, recreation centers, community parks, bicycle lanes, walking paths, golf courses, churches, day care centers, and commercial and retail areas in a cost-effective and cost-efficient design that is constructed with minimum financial impact on taxpayers.

In 1988, Hawaii led the nation in home ownership and rental housing costs. With only 44% of Hawaii's households in home ownership, Hawaii lagged behind the national average by approximately 20%. In the summer of 1990, the average four-member Oahu family made $41,200 a year, giving them the purchasing power to buy a $128,000 home. During that same period, the median resale price for a home in Hawaii was $350,000.

The reduction of federal funding for lower-income housing, the lack of existing infrastructure (water, sewer, drainage, utilities, roads) and suitable land for development, the high amount of required capital for infrastructure development and the associated financial risks, and the high cost of construction financing caused a widening gap between housing supply and housing demand during the late 1970s and 1980s. True, the private sector and city and state governments were building homes, but these were relatively small, "in-fill" type projects that relied on existing infrastructure. HFDC estimated that by the year 2000, the demand for housing would reach over 85,000 units, with 64,000 of these units having to be affordable to households with average or below average incomes. Besides the need for significant numbers of affordable housing, there was also the desire to avoid creating massive affordable housing "projects" that could lead to further social ills. To address this, the decision was made to create quality lifestyle communities.

It was recognized that the state was facing severe budget constraints and that taxpayers could not bear the full cost of funding the required affordable housing. Consequently, another objective was to build a significant number of homes efficiently through economies of scale and to fund this in a way that would minimize the economic impact to taxpayers.

The Master Planned Communities are producing a significant number of homes, 4,000 to 5,000 per MPC on each island. Because of the scale, housing can be put in quicker and cheaper per home unit. In addition, current and future community needs (schools, roads, drainage, parks, commercial and retail areas) are anticipated, planned, and prepared. The projects deliver housing for a range of needs: for singles, single-parent families, and families there are for-sale townhouses and single-family homes, self-help and owner-builder housing, and moderate- to low-income rentals. Also, for those who are elderly, physically challenged, or both, each community features rental apartments. Finally, development of homes by private industry is facilitated through HFDC overall planning, zoning, infrastructure development, and provision of financial incentives.

The program creates a significant number of homes (13,400) in quality lifestyle communities rather than producing limited numbers of units in traditional in-fill housing projects. The effort addresses a cross-section of the population in need (60% of Hawaii's households) and creates socioeconomically balanced communities. The program minimizes the impact to taxpayers through the use of revolving funds, bond financing, lease and sale of commercial and retail areas, and the Shared Appreciation Program. It features antispeculative and equity-sharing provisions in the form of "buyback" and shared appreciation programs. Finally, the concept encourages private sector development of affordable housing by directly removing local barriers.

The *Greensboro [North Carolina] Affordable Housing Vision* is funded by the Greensboro Housing Partnership Trust Fund, which was created by the allocation of one cent of the city's ad valorem tax for the exclusive use of affordable housing initiatives. This unique funding program grew out of the community's awareness of the need for affordable housing in Greensboro and its commitment to fund this prioritized need. Working with a budget of approximately $1 million annually, the city's special division of housing development has acted as partner, facilitator, and catalyst, uniting diverse groups in this effort.

The goal of Greensboro's Affordable Housing Vision is to provide decent, affordable, safe housing to all of its citizens within this generation. In 1989, a goal was set of having 500 families living in affordable housing by 1995. In just 3 years, 680 homes were either completed or well under way. The Partnership invested $7,641,831 of public funds and generated $26,203,474 in private capital for a total of $33,845,305 in new or rehabilitated housing. This program emphasizes public-private partnerships with both nonprofit and for-profit developers to provide housing to those earning 30% to 50% of the area's median income.

The *City of Greenville Home Ownership Program,* South Carolina, has addressed the decreasing supply of quality housing in low-income areas over a period of several years, countering deterioration by facilitating private home ownership. As the housing conditions deteriorated, owner occupants moved away from the areas. Disinvestment continued and housing conditions became progressively worse in the community. A related problem was the conversion of homes from owner occupancy to rental units, creating a vicious cycle of deterioration.

Greenville developed a public-private venture that provides for the construction of modestly priced houses for purchase by low-income citizens. The program combines Federal Community Development Fund dollars for the down payment and site improvement assistance, below-market financing for home buyers provided through the South Carolina State Housing Authority, competitive bidding for home construction to control the purchase price ($30,000), and affordable monthly payments ($236.06) for program participants.

The program, sponsored and coordinated by the city's Community Development Department, has been operating for 4 years, has produced 22 new homes in two different communities (a total of 38 are planned), and has made a significant contribution to neighborhood stabilization and revitalization. The city has approximately $10,000 invested in each home (no owner has defaulted on mortgage payments or has been delinquent) and believes that it has received significant returns on that investment: (a) Low-income families gain a new home that they otherwise would never have been able to afford; (b) their children thrive on the stability provided by growing up in a home in which the head of the household is working to purchase the home; (c) new houses help stabilize and revitalize the neighborhoods, which in turn stimulates private investment; (d) the city government gains a new tax base and a solid core of people dedicated to maintaining and improving the quality of life in city neighborhoods; and (e) housing contractors benefit, because the program supports small business.

Housing Vermont is a statewide, nonprofit corporation created by the Vermont Housing Agency in 1988 to preserve and/or develop affordable rental housing for its citizens. The program was also established to foster innovative relationships between public and private interests in Vermont, in response to the need for affordable housing.

This program primarily serves low- and moderate-income families in Vermont who will most benefit from affordable rental housing. The development effort was made possible by the formation of Housing Vermont, which deviates from other similar development projects. An important and innovative component is the Vermont Equity Fund, an investment vehicle designed to give corporate investors an opportunity for relatively low-risk investments in housing. Housing Vermont encourages private corporations to invest in affordable housing in exchange for Low-income housing tax credits. The value of these credits has increased by 30% over a traditional syndication through the efforts of the issuer. The Equity Fund is the first investment vehicle of its kind supported by a state housing finance agency. Within its first 2 years of operation, Housing Vermont witnessed the completion of 700 units of perpetually affordable housing, representing a highly effective partnership between public and private interests. The program has also committed an additional $4.9 million of equity toward the creation of 328 units of housing in three developments of mixed income, senior, and family housing. There also exists a commitment to rehabilitate a significant stock of existing housing in Vermont that is at risk of being converted to market rents. Housing Vermont also acts as a developer, which translates into significant cost savings for each project undertaken. As an arm of the Vermont Housing Finance Agency, Housing Vermont is a statewide public entity, yet because it functions at the operational level, it has more flexibility and independence than a traditional state agency. With some legal and administrative hurdles to overcome, Housing Vermont is a program likely to be successful in other large municipalities or at the state level. It stresses local involvement in the issue of affordable housing, the assurance of perpetual affordability, and a commitment to work closely with private interests and developers.

Meeting Company Needs. The *Governor's Guaranteed Work Force Program (GGWPF)* in the state of West Virginia is designed to assist both new companies entering the state and existing companies to meet new competitive or technological needs. The program provides up to $1,000 of training per employee per year, and will guarantee the training to the satisfaction of the employer for up to an additional $1,000 of training per employee per year. To access the program, existing companies must create at least 10 new jobs within a 12-month period. The GGWFP works with each company individually to structure the highest-quality training program possible. The GGWFP customizes training programs to meet each company's goals and requirements. A variety of different types of training could be provided, including the following: basic skills (such as reading, mathematics, or computer literacy), job-specific technical skills, employee involvement, and managerial training. The office works with each of the specific training providers to ensure that the training will be performed at the lowest possible cost to the taxpayer. For example, whereas the office is legally permitted to provide up to $1,000 of assistance per employee, in FY 91 high-quality, cost-effective training was provided at an average cost of $327.12 per trainee. The program provides the opportunity for businesses to become more competitive, thereby increasing the vitality and economic viability of the state's communities. Through better skilled, more highly productive workers, companies are more able to adapt to new business challenges and to compete with companies from around the world.

Insuring Everyone's Healthcare. Prior to passage of the *State Health Insurance Program (SHIP)* in 1989, an estimated population of 30,000 medically uninsured Hawaiians avoided seeking care during early stages of illness due to inability to pay costs. Through a partnership of the state and the private sector, and sliding-scale premiums for members, the program now subsidizes residents who did not previously qualify for any form of health insurance.

With SHIP, Hawaii's health care system provides universal access to basic primary preventive health care. SHIP subsidizes health care insurance for Hawaiians whose gross family income does not exceed 300% of the federal poverty level, who are ineligible for other government programs, and who have no employer-based insurance. The five major areas of coverage are preventive, outpatient, emergency, maternity, and hospital inpatient services. In 2 years, more than 15,000 members have been enrolled; there is a statewide network of volunteer SHIP registrars; a major provider has decreased premium rates; increased benefits have been added; and no-cost linkages with other services have been established.

Partnering for Care. The New York state (NYS) *Partnership for Long Term Care,* implemented in 1993, emphasizes shared responsibility for financing long-term care (LTC) by offering New Yorkers an alternative way to pay for their LTC. The Partnership encourages middle-income citizens to purchase long-term health care insurance coverage as protection against impoverishment.

New York state nursing home costs are among the highest in the nation, with an average monthly charge in excess of $5,333. Before the Partnership, New Yorkers faced a Hobson's choice: pay out-of-pocket and risk impoverishment, or transfer assets to appear impoverished. Regardless of the route to impoverishment, people come into the Medicaid program, which then pays for their LTC at taxpayers' expense.

The Partnership targets middle-income citizens for participation based on the rationale that while they cannot pay for long-term health care services, they could afford quality long-term care insurance coverage. The Partnership provides a disincentive for purchasers to rely primarily on Medicaid to pay for their LTC by offering "total asset protection." Purchasers qualify for Medicaid eligibility after approved LTC insurance benefits are exhausted. The premise of the Partnership is that it holds the potential of significant savings compared to the Medicaid program over time as more people, who would have spent down or transferred assets absent the program, purchase LTC insurance. The core resource of the Partnership is the cooperative relationship between participating insurance companies and the New York state government.

Solving Common Problems. The *Salt Lake County Business/Government Alliance* is a public-private partnership composed of business community members and members from Salt Lake County government that plans, studies, and implements solutions to common problems facing the county and business. In today's complex and highly technical society, the business/government combination represents a unique method of solving community problems without costly consultant fees. Private business managers and executives bring valuable private sector expertise and knowledge—pro bono—to county government decision making. The value of private sector volunteers serving as members of a business-government alliance (BGA) and its task forces was calculated to be $172,400, based on a standard hourly rate of $40.

The creation of task forces and subcommittees of the BGA enlarges the circle of participation for Salt Lake County residents. Many more citizens, professionals and nonprofessionals in the private sector are provided an opportunity to play an important role in shaping county government decisions. These task forces and subcommittees effectively help promote and maintain "open door government."

During its existence, the Business/Government Alliance has studied and made recommendations to Salt Lake County in a wide variety of areas. These recommendations have aided in policy decisions and improved efficiencies in Salt Lake County government. The BGA has closely examined and made recommendations for Salt Lake County in facilities planning, water management, the Salt Palace (county-owned sports arena), the form of county government, the criminal justice system, the county tax system, county government roles and revenues, and transportation solutions.

Cooperating Across Sectors. New York state's *Self-Help Support System* is a joint partnership of the state's departments of state, environmental conservation, and health; the Environmental Facilities Corporation; and The Rensselaerville Institute. This innovative and dynamic technical assistance team, the only public-private coalition of its kind in the country, provides expertise to alleviate water and wastewater problems of small communities.

The need for improvement in water and wastewater systems is well documented. In New York state water systems alone, reliable estimates put capital needs at over 6 billion dollars (in 1980 dollars). Rural systems (serving 10,000 people or less) account for 1.2 billion of this total. For wastewater systems, the situation is even worse. Documented needs exceed $10.2 billion, with another $3.75 billion estimated. Despite the need, federal and state programs do not provide sufficient funds to solve these problems—especially in smaller, rural communities.

Self-help is an important alternative for many communities with urgent needs and very limited financial resources. Self-help begins with the idea that local communities have traditionally done many things for themselves, recognizing the principle that the best way to get money is to need less of it.

Since its inception, the Self-Help Support System's small staff of five has provided technical assistance to 316 towns and villages as a field-operations-style program. This effort has generated 113 construction projects, saving New York state's communities $15 million.

NOT-FOR-PROFIT PARTNERS

The public sector has a long history of cooperative relationships with the nonprofit sector, particularly in the field of health and human services.

Protecting Children's Health. The Medical Care for Children Project (MCCP) in Fairfax County, Virginia, is a public-private partnership that provides low-cost medical services to children from indigent families that lack Medicaid, health insurance, cash, or any other resources to pay for health care. It is significant in that it successfully addresses a problem of growing proportions, namely, how can the needs of the medically indigent be met in times of fiscal austerity?

MCCP has two components: (a) acute care, which consists of services for acute illnesses provided by private physicians and medical laboratories at a cost to the clients of $1 per service; and (b) comprehensive services, which consist of preventive, general care, inpatient, physical therapy, mental health, and pharmacy services provided by a health maintenance organization at no cost to clients. Nonprofit community organizations identify eligible children, broker and arrange the services (e.g., recruitment of physicians, client appointments, transportation), and process payments.

The primary goal of the program is to reduce the incidence and consequences of late, inadequate, or nontreatment of children's illnesses by increasing the number of poor children receiving low-or no-cost pediatric services, increasing the number of health care providers who deliver services to low-income children at reduced or no cost, and increasing the continuity of health care for low-income children. A related goal is to facilitate family efforts to become self-supporting by increasing a family's resources for food, clothing, and shelter, and by reducing costs for health care, transportation, and other medical costs. The children to be served are identified in their community through neighborhood organizations that broker medical services for clients and also assist the families in obtaining other resources, such as clothing, job training, job search assistance, and emergency food.

MCCP departs from previous programs in that it serves children who are not eligible for other programs or who have medical needs that are not met by public or private agencies. The County Health Department, for example, limits its services to preventive care such as blood pressure screening, immunizations, and care for handicapping conditions. MCCP provides health services to indigent children at minimal cost:

1. Physicians will provide services at 50% of usual charges.
2. HMOs are willing to reduce costs for comprehensive care.
3. Other health care providers, such as medical laboratories and pharmacies, will provide services at 50% of usual charges or at cost.
4. To reduce costs further, county and community organizations tap existing community resources for medical care (e.g., the Lions Club for funds to pay for eye care, the American Cancer Society for screenings).

Recruiting Inmates as Allies. Until an alliance was formed between the county's Intermediate Unit, the Bucks County Correction Facility, and the county's Lion and Lioness Clubs, blind students in Bucks County, Pennsylvania, found it very difficult to excel in regular classes because of a lack of adequate braille materials. Teachers had to spend inordinate amounts of time to braille textbooks and other materials needed by blind students. Under the *Brailling Texts* program, funds from the Lion/Lioness Clubs allowed the acquisition of special software and computer hardware, which is housed in the Correctional Facility. Now inmates, instead of teachers, braille textbooks, workbooks, and dittos. This cooperative effort not only increased the involvement and productivity of blind students, but also the productivity of inmates involved in the project. Teachers now have more time to dedicate to classroom teaching and inmates are learning a valuable skill.

Preserving Lands. The Palm Beach County *Environmentally Sensitive Lands Acquisition Program* was developed in response to citizen concerns that environmentally sensitive lands in the county were rapidly being lost to development. These lands contain native plant communities, wildlife populations, endangered plant and animal species, and water recharge areas.

The voters of Palm Beach County passed a $100 million bond issue to fund the acquisition of approximately 25,000 acres of environmentally sensitive lands. Soon after the bond issue was passed, the county entered into a unique contract with The Nature Conservancy to provide a variety of services related to the acquisition and management of these lands. County staff conducted biological evaluations of the sites to be acquired, prepared grant applications, provided staff support for advisory committee meetings and site visits, and performed all real estate-related activities to complete the acquisitions. The Nature Conservancy conducted all landowner contact and negotiation activities, reported its progress to the advisory committee, and provided the benefits of its expertise in many areas to the county.

This public-private partnership between the county and The Nature Conservancy has resulted in a savings of $25,061,000 on the purchase of lands with an appraised value of $54,494,000. Because of joint efforts by the county's Department of Environmental Resources Management (ERM) and Nature Conservancy staff, 11 of the 15 high-priority sites received approval for state matching funds. Three of these sites were joint acquisitions with the City of Boca Raton, which provided municipal matching funds from its $12 million bond issue to fund the acquisition of sites in Boca Raton. The partnership between the county and The Nature Conservancy has enabled the county to leverage its funds so that up to $150 million worth of environmentally sensitive lands can be purchased with the initial $100 million bond issue.

As the county purchases these high-priority sites, ERM will manage the lands as nature preserves in perpetuity. The public will be encouraged to use the lands for passive recreational activities, scientific research, education, and environmental awareness.

Developing Public Policy. The *Trenton Office of Policy Studies (TOPS)* was created by the City of Trenton, New Jersey, and Thomas Edison State College as an innovative partnership bringing together the best insights of the academic community and the public and private sectors in order to address vital, emerging public policy issues facing the City of Trenton. TOPS was designed to be proactive in assisting the city government in formulating programs and plans to address these issues. In carrying out its responsibilities, TOPS draws upon the expertise of faculty, staff, and students associated with Trenton-area institutions of higher education, public policy practitioners, and other appropriate consultants. TOPS has grown to include participation by each of the surrounding institutions of higher learning, as well as representatives of community groups, businesses, and other concerned institutions.

Coordinating Care. Hudson County, New Jersey, has the second highest per capita incidence of HIV/AIDS in the country. The *Hudson County AIDS Network of Care* responds to the epidemic through a coordinated system of care. A case management approach is incorporated to reduce the fragmentation of care that usually exists within a countywide service delivery system. The network provides for an early detection and treatment program for individuals infected with HIV. A systems approach that utilizes community partnerships within the county and among the diverse municipalities enhances the quality of services provided and reduces the costs associated with delivering such high-level services.

Under this project, a consortium of nonprofit health care and human services providers was created to promote a cooperative spirit, rather than a competitive one, that would provide the most comprehensive system of care possible to needy residents of Hudson County. Grassroots planning and the involvement of community groups since the onset of the program minimized fear and NIMBY ("not in my back yard") attitudes among county residents. This grassroots planning ensured the development of a countywide network of care that is culturally responsive to and reflective of the ethnically diverse community.

CONCLUSION

Creative partnerships—with other levels of government, with the private sector, with nonprofit agencies—illustrate how a wide range of stakeholders can develop, deliver, and sustain public programs. The examples presented in this chapter touch on the various reasons why partnerships are formed: to address complex social issues that one agency alone could not possibly handle and to reduce, and if possible alleviate, the fragmentation and duplication that exist in the service delivery system. All of these partnerships realize cost savings while at the same time tangibly improving the quality of services provided.

Innovative partnerships between the public and private sectors, and across agencies, departments, levels, and even branches of the government, serve as models for significantly higher levels of accomplishment once we begin to think outside the normal bureaucratic box. Federal, state, and local governments need to encourage and support effective partnerships that improve service delivery, reduce expenses, and overcome fragmentation and duplication of government functions. When permitted to approach problem-solving creatively, public servants can create exciting programs, producing more productive, more responsive government.

REFERENCES

■

Barnekov, T. K., & Raffel, J. (1992). Public management of privatization. In M. Holzer (Ed.), *Public productivity handbook* (pp. 99-115). New York: Marcel Dekker.

Donahue, J. D. (1984). *The privatization decision: Public ends, private means.* New York: Basic Books.

Katz, J. I. (1991, June). Privatizing without tears. *Governing Magazine*, pp. 38-42.

Ogilvy, J. A. (1986-1987, Winter). Scenarios for the future of governance. *The Bureaucrat*, pp. 13-16.

Savas, E. S. (1987). *Privatization: The key to better government.* Chatham, NJ: Chatham House.

Savas, E. S. (1992). Privatization and productivity. In M. Holzer (Ed.), *Public productivity handbook* (pp. 79-99). New York: Marcel Dekker.

Stahl, O. G. (1988, Summer). What's missing in privatization. *The Bureaucrat*, pp. 41-44.

6

MEASUREMENT FOR PERFORMANCE

■

Measuring Performance and Evaluation

Establishing Goals and Measuring Results ──
Estimating and Justifying Resource Requirements ──
Reallocating Resources ──
Developing Organization Improvement Strategies ──
Motivating Employees to Improve Performance ──┘

MEASURES CLARIFY ACCOMPLISHMENTS

■────────────────────────────────

Although public servants produce necessary public services, their agencies have not always built a capacity for measurement that can highlight both progress and the need for critical investments. Faced with competing demands and expectations, public sector agencies confront issues that seem to defy measurement. Without the pressure of competition or the "unforgiving bottom line" of profit and loss, governmental agencies are likely to ignore performance measurement as they focus on more pressing issues (Ammons, 1996, p. 9). In light of the growing emphasis on controlling costs, maintaining accountability, and reducing the size of government, performance measurement has become a priority in many state and local agencies.

Performance measurement provides governments with a means of keeping score on how well their various departments and operations are doing. As Hatry (1978) notes, scorekeeping is essential:

> Unless you are keeping score, it is difficult to know whether you are winning or losing. This applies to ball games, card games, and no less government productivity. . . . Productivity measurements permit governments to identify problem areas and, as corrective actions are taken, to detect the extent to which improvements have occurred. (p. 28)

Measurement of performance has always been implicit in questions as to outputs and outcomes: Is crime up? Are the streets cleaner? Is the air quality better? How well are our children doing in school? In short, is a program producing as promised? The answers to such questions are important. They can provide feedback that influences decisions to allocate or reallocate public sector resources, to set or change priorities. Such decisions are made "internally" by public managers, chief executives and legislators. They are substantially influenced "externally" by feedback from citizens, public interest-advocate groups, private businesses, and their elected or media surrogates. Each of these actors—internal or external—holds opinions as to service priorities.

Following the "subjective" arrow in Figure 7.1 (on p. 134 of next chapter), however, it can be seen that opinions as to the allocation of scare public resources are often based upon vague assessments of efficiency and efficacy, judgments that are typically subjective and "soft." They may be formed from a critical incident of success or failure. They may be grounded in a rumor. They may be a function of a personal experience.

But following the "objective" arrow in Figure 7.1, we see that performance measurement offers an opportunity to develop and present "hard" data instead. Measurement provides an opportunity to present evidence that the public sector is a public bargain; to highlight the routine, but important, services that public servants quietly provide; to answer the public's sometimes angry questions and implicit suggestions on a dispassionate basis. Measurement, then, helps to move the basis of decision making from personal experience to measurable accomplishment (or lack thereof). Data about levels and trends of outputs and outcomes, and associated benefit/cost ratios, helps defend, expand, or improve a program, rather than proceeding from relatively subjective, political decisions based on circumstantial (if any) evidence. Measurement helps answer objectively such questions as: Is an organization doing its job? Is it creating unintended side effects or producing unanticipated impacts? Is it responsive to the public? Is it fair to all, or does it favor certain groups, inadvertently or deliberately? Does it keep within its proper bounds of authorized activity? In short, is it productive?

In the process of providing answers to those questions, productive governments stress multiple measures: internal capacities, outputs produced, and outcomes achieved.

1. High-performing public organizations monitor the production of internal services that contribute to the efficient and effective production of external services for clients. Such internal (or "invisible") services as maintenance, training, and auditing are necessary prerequisites to the production of outputs.

2. Outputs are measurable as services provided in terms of such factors as quantity (How many clients are served? How many units of service are delivered?) and quality (Are the services delivered to certain standards? What is the error rate?)

3. *Output,* however, is a narrow term that limits interpretations of productivity improvement. If managers are to make better decisions as to resource allocation and reallocation, then they need not only measures of outputs but also of "outcomes"—what services result in, such as improvements in a client's quality of life or ability to maintain employment (i.e., the accomplishments of programs as described in Chapter 2, Management for Quality).

MEASURES ARE AVAILABLE

A productive agency must, therefore, monitor and improve productivity at all three stages—internal services, external services, and outcomes—and communicate those measures clearly and honestly to the public. Fortunately, the tools are available. Performance measurement is fairly well developed as a set of tools for making better decisions within public organizations. Managers who are responsible for day-to-day management now often have access to information that helps them implement public policies effectively and efficiently. A substantial body of research demonstrates that measurement of public services is conceptually sound and feasible. For example, the Government Accomplishment and Accountability Task Force of the American Society for Public

Administration (1996) has produced an extensive manual titled *Perform-ance Measurement Training.*

Overall, then, a measurement program, which requires substantial expertise and careful planning, can ask, and begin to answer, such questions as those in Exhibit 6.1.

EXHIBIT 6.1
SAMPLE PERFORMANCE
MEASUREMENT QUESTIONS

In terms of program performance:

> How much of a service is provided?
> How efficiently are resources used?
> How effectively is a service provided?

In terms of effectiveness indicators for performance:

> What is the intended purpose of the service?
> What are the unintended impacts of the service?
> How effective is the service in prevention of problems before they arise?
> Is the service adequate?
> Is the service accessible?
> Are clients satisfied with services?
> Are services distributed equitably?
> Is a product durable?
> To what extent is a service provided to clients in a manner that maintains their dignity?

In terms of desirable characteristics of performance measures:

> Is a service significant?
> Is the service appropriate to the problem being addressed?
> Is performance quantifiable?
> Are services readily available?
> Are services delivered in a timely manner?
> Are services delivered in a relatively straightforward manner?
> Is a measure of performance valid?

Is a measure acceptable?
Is performance measured completely?
Are measures accurate?
Are measures reliable?

MEASURES HELP IMPROVE DECISIONS

Public managers and policymakers have the performance measurement tools to help carry out their responsibilities to deliver and improve services, as promised, in at least eight different ways (Hatry & Fisk, 1992):

■ Establishing goals and measuring results
■ Estimating and justifying resource requirements
■ Reallocating resources
■ Developing organization improvement strategies
■ Motivating employees to improve performance
■ Controlling operations
■ Predicting periods of work overload or underload
■ Developing more sophisticated capacities for measurement

EXSL award winning programs provide evidence that they do so.

ESTABLISHING GOALS AND MEASURING RESULTS

The need to "hold programs accountable" is a popular and political prescription. But accountable for what? To the extent that goals are vague, the public will be neither satisfied nor informed as to progress (or lack thereof). The best public programs specify goals, treat those goals as planned targets, and match results with plans. Such comparisons facilitate accountability.

Preventing Pregnancies. Under the auspices of the Office of Minority Health/Division of Health Education and Information, the Richmond (Virginia) City Health Department has made teen pregnancy prevention a focal point. A *Campaign to Save Our Children: Teen Pregnancy Prevention Project (TPPP)* effectively initiated a highly visible media campaign to keep the prevention and abstinence message in the public eye. Richmond's campaign focuses on delaying sexual initiation by teenagers by effectively utilizing a media campaign; increasing access to family planning services for sexually active teens by expanding adolescent clinics; increasing support to parents as the sexuality educators of their children through specific health education programs; and increasing the general public's and policymakers' awareness of teenage pregnancy by expanding the community outreach program. The well-organized education initiative serves to enhance the family-based knowledge of prevention and continues to provide support to the family through the use of bus placards, newspaper info ads, the *Aftermath* comic book, T-shirts, and radio commercials that include contests. The objectives of the project have been realized through a collaborative effort of agencies, churches, organizations, and citizens, and the entire community has been receptive and responsive to the efforts of the department.

The goal of the pregnancy prevention project is to reduce the number of teenage pregnancies and specifically teen pregnancy among girls 19 years and under to no more than 83 per 1,000 female adolescents. At the outset of the project, the Richmond city teen pregnancy rate was more than 100 per 1,000 female adolescents, or almost double that of the state. In the project's first year, the city nearly met the stated goal, experiencing a decline in the rate to 86 per 1,000, at a saving in medical expenses of almost $20,000 per birth. The use of performance measures was necessary to the program's continued funding: providing evidence of progress toward the program's goal, helping build continued support for the program, and underscoring the high benefit-to-cost ratio.

Increasing Home Ownership. Milwaukee had a reputation as one of the most segregated communities in the country. It was identified as having the highest ratio in the nation of mortgage rejections for blacks as compared to whites. Home ownership rates were declining and market deterioration was widespread and escalating. These conditions were accompanied by an increase in poverty, unemployment, and crime in the area. As social problems escalated, property values deteriorated, making lending even more difficult and disinvestment more likely.

In 1990, the Wisconsin Housing and Economic Development Authority (WHEDA) began work with city officials, lenders, real estate professionals, and community leaders to increase home ownership in the central city by creating the *Heart of Milwaukee Initiative.* The program was designed to gain the support of city officials as well as community leaders to promote home ownership in an effort to stabilize the core of the city. WHEDA recognized that the keys to expanded opportunities for minorities are affordable financing and home buyer education. The support of local lending institutions was secured in order to provide affordable financing for minorities interested in purchasing homes in the central city. Financing includes low interest rate mortgages with down payments of as little as 5%, and loans to help low-income families finance the costs of closing a mortgage. As one measure, the WHEDA home buyer seminar series has provided education to more than 5,000 Milwaukee residents since 1990. Another bottom-line measure was a dramatic increase in lending in the central city, from 58 loans in 1989 to 216 in 1992. Both methods more than doubled expected goals.

Measuring Outcomes. The *Program Measurement System* of St. Petersburg, Florida, was designed and implemented as a multifaceted data-based system of analysis of governmental performance in terms of program outcome measures. The goal of this system is to provide information to policymakers in three areas: management, budgeting, and accountability.

The system is a systematic approach to objectively obtaining and evaluating information regarding the performance of city programs against established objectives. It requires city management to focus on results rather than activities. The system is designed to focus on service outcomes rather than agency output or workload measures. All programs are approached from the perspective of their ultimate impact on the citizen.

Management team and departmental personnel are able to make more informed decisions, as well as informing the public of the degree of accomplishment of city programs. It is a centrally coordinated system that provides analysis and support to department personnel and identifies potential problems and areas of opportunities to the management team. The program offers three separate components:

1. The Program Measurement System is a step-by-step approach to the development of a mission statement, goals, objectives, and measures for each program of government.
2. Minisurveys allow a government to get direct information from its "clients" on how well it is doing on a regular basis, data that is essential to assessing the effectiveness of its programs.

3. The Focus Group is a structured approach involving the use of "internal consultants" to target problem areas or programs that need improvement.

The focus group component of the Program Measurement System has had the most immediate impact on cost savings, revenue increases, and improved services. In the Occupational Tax Section, the focus group analyzed revenue and field hours, and recommended the creation of an additional inspector position. This investment was recovered in less than 3 months through increased revenue collection and now contributes an additional $100,000 per year in increased occupational tax revenue. Another focus group that was formed to study the city's Consolidated Warehouse made recommendations that resulted in improvements that turned an operating deficit of $10,000 a month to an operating profit of $7,000 a month and reduced the overhead from 21% to 19% in only one year.

ESTIMATING AND JUSTIFYING
RESOURCE REQUIREMENTS

Budgets are estimates of resource requirements. Traditionally, they are based on past expenditures and "guesstimates" as to future needs. But fiscal planning can be accomplished more systematically and quantitatively. Justifications as to expenditures can be more precise, more objective, and more factual to the extent that they are the products of measurement.

Capital Budgeting. New Castle County, Delaware, has developed and implemented a *Capital Strategies and Review System (CAPSTARS)* program to evaluate ongoing capital projects and analyze the capital planning process. The program provides a useful quantitative tool for strategic/fiscal planning, for authorizing capital projects, and for maintaining a continuous capital program cycle throughout the year. In addition, CAPSTARS provides more timely and accurate planning and fiscal information to management, legislators, and the general public.

Results achieved through the implementation of CAPSTARS include seven key quantitative fiscal measures that assess the impact of capital projects on the county's operating budget. CAPSTARS has helped assess the cost-effectiveness of major, ongoing capital projects. The program also establishes a necessary linkage between the capital program and the operating budget, a linkage that is often overlooked.

REALLOCATING RESOURCES

Measurement contributes to more productive resource allocation decisions. It may help save substantial sums by developing and evaluating benefit-cost linkages. It may help reduce costs by highlighting lower-cost alternatives.

Reevaluating Costs. Value Engineering (VE) is a tool for evaluating the cost-effectiveness, reliability, quality, and safety of design projects. The *Clean Water Program (CWP)* of San Diego retains qualified consultants, each an expert in his or her field, to perform a VE study on projects that include the design of pipelines, water reclamation plants, secondary wastewater treatment plants, and sludge processing facilities. The main objective is to evaluate proposed design and related cost estimates submitted to the city by designers. VE studies are intended to ensure that performance, reliability, quality, and safety are provided at the lowest possible life-cycle cost. During one 3-month period, for example, the CWP conducted nine VE studies at a total cost of $824,000. The exercise resulted in changes in design and modification of cost estimates that yielded savings of more than $70 million, for an overall savings-to-fee ratio of 85:1.

Each VE study typically proceeds in four stages:

1. Pre-workshop: This involves gathering all pertinent information; developing strategies; and preparing cost, energy, and life-cycle models.
2. Workshop: The VE team develops cost-saving ideas for design alternatives within established constraints.
3. Post-workshop: The designer reviews and responds to the VE team ideas with recommendations to accept or reject. The city staff reviews both proposed VE ideas and designer's responses. Then, at the VE Team Implementation meeting, a joint meeting between the VE leader, the designer, and the city staff, decisions are made by the city on which recommendations are to be implemented.
4. Report: The results of the VE study are presented in a report that includes a description of each recommendation (i.e., a summary of the preliminary design and proposed changes, a comparison of cost estimates, and a detailed discussion on the advantages and disadvantages of each recommendation).

The report also contains the city's decision on either accepting or rejecting each recommendation.

Decreasing Costs. The Town of Culpepper, Virginia, improved its insurance and *Risk Management Program* over a 4-year period as against a base year. Measurable factors should have caused insurance and risk management costs to increase significantly: Prior to the initiation of this program the town's worker compensation costs were escalating sharply, it was in an assigned risk pool and injuries were mounting, other types of insurance were not being properly analyzed, coverages were deficient in some areas, and no attention was being given to safety practices and risk management control.

The report of the risk management project graphically depicts reductions that actually occurred. This report contrasts the factors that impact the cost of insurance, the steps taken to implement a cost-effective risk management program, and the positive results achieved. The town saved $237,130 over the 4-year period and reduced its insurance cost by 39.1%. The report also explains the procedures, steps, and techniques employed to implement the program. A formal safety policy and a loss control/safety manual have been adopted. Supervisors now have a better understanding of the risk management program, the benefits to be derived from a formal safety program, and the necessity for improved employee safety in the workplace.

DEVELOPING ORGANIZATION
IMPROVEMENT STRATEGIES

Measures can help bring problems into focus. Once clear, problems can then be addressed in a more systematic manner, such as overcoming obstacles, targeting services, and planning for anticipated problems. In short, measurement can help avoid disappointments and surprises.

Lowering Barriers. In 1988, the San Joaquin County (California) Maternal Child Adolescent Health Advisory Board identified seven serious county barriers to care: insufficient number of facilities in locations frequented by target groups; financial constraints, including inadequate insurance or public funds; uneven availability of services, particularly to disadvantaged or high-risk women; limited transportation services; disorganized and uncoordinated outreach efforts to recruit hard-to-reach women; negative experiences, attitudes, and beliefs of women seeking care; and child care deficiencies.

By utilizing resources available through the County Health Care Services as well as support from 15 other public and private service providers, the San Joaquin County Hospital moved to eliminate these barriers under its *Comprehensive System of Maternal/Infant Services*. The outcomes included the design and implementation of a Prenatal Care and Public Education Program, the expansion of the Healthy Beginnings Clinics, the initiation of a Comprehensive Perinatal Services Program (CPSP), the design and implementation of an Incentives Program that rewards pregnant and postpartum women for keeping medical appointments, the design and implementation of programs for substance abusing pregnant and postpartum women, and the development and implementation of the Black Women's Program.

Since the implementation of CPSP, "no show" rates for clinic appointments have decreased from 33% to less than 10%. One group of substance-abusing women in the program achieved a 95% attendance rate for assessments and classes. Successful attendance resulted in higher than expected birth weights for the babies of these mothers and a smaller number of toxicology screen positive babies born. The incentives program offers positive behavior reinforcement as well as goods and services for the time participants invest in keeping appointments and going to classes.

Success for substance-abusing women has also been impressive: 82% of the initial postpartum group completed the program and 80% maintained sobriety for at least 3 months after completion. Smaller numbers of babies are admitted to neonatal intensive care units, smaller numbers of babies are born addicted to cocaine and heroin, and larger numbers of women begin prenatal care early in their pregnancy and faithfully continue that care throughout their pregnancy.

Building a Database. The Somerset County (New Jersey) Youth Services Commission developed the *Adolescent Information Form (AIF)* as a comprehensive, cross-system data collection mechanism to profile troubled adolescents. The form is a simple, one-page descriptive document that is completed at intake on every child between the ages of 10 and 18. These forms are collected monthly from the 28 agencies across Somerset County that use them, and forwarded to the commission's office, where they are entered into a master database. Reports are then generated to summarize data on all youth, for example, between certain ages, or those with a history of foster care or poor school performance. The reports are also used to track youths through the juvenile system and as a basis for individualized profiles.

The AIF has had a direct, positive impact on the planning process for youth and their families in the county, helping the agency plan for future services; integrating information across agencies, it makes available reports based on hard data in contrast to individual perceptions or impressions of how the system is functioning. Other county agencies also use the information gathered by the commission.

Planning for Growth. The city of Carlsbad, California, has grown very quickly, doubling in population during the 1980s, with an average annual growth rate of as much as 10%, and it is continuing to grow in the 1990s. Citizens complained of congested streets, lack of parks, and overcrowded schools.

The Carlsbad City Council, staff, citizens, and development community worked together to design and implement a program that would effectively address the concerns of all parties. The *Carlsbad Growth Management Program* is an effective approach to managing city growth by ensuring the adequacy of public facilities and services. An essential feature of the program is its use of public facility performance standards and its comprehensive, detail-oriented approach to facility planning and financing. Through implementation of the program, the city has developed a way to ensure that adequate public facilities and services will be provided concurrent with the demand created by growth. The program goal is to manage residential, commercial, and industrial growth based upon compliance with 11 facility-based performance standards.

The program uses a three-tiered comprehensive planning approach:

1. Under a citywide facilities and improvements plan, it adopted 11 public facility performance standards, divided the city into 25 Facility Management Zones, inventoried existing citywide public facilities, and projected public facility needs.

2. Through local facility management zone plans, the city implemented the provisions of the Growth Management Plan, which was prepared by property owners within each of the 25 zones, phased in all development and public facility needs in accordance with the growth management plan, and planned for financing mechanisms to provide for the public facilities.

3. Individual development projects were required to comply with the provisions of the Local Facilities Management Plan and to implement the provisions of the Citywide Facilities and Improvements Plans.

In the first 3 years of implementation of the growth management plan, measurable accomplishments included the following:

1. Fourteen of the 25 zones in the city adopted local facilities management plans.

2. One new community park was developed, and the entire acreage for another community park was dedicated as a unit rather than piecemeal (as was done previously).

3. A citywide traffic analysis was prepared, and an annual monitoring program was put in place to measure ongoing service levels of all major roads and intersections.

4. Major road improvements were implemented.

5. A financing plan was adopted to fund improvements to the three freeway interchanges in the city.

6. A new fire station was constructed and another was under construction.

7. A site was acquired to build a new branch library.

8. The city adopted a long-range, 25-year, build-out capital improvement program (CIP) rather than the previous, limited, 5-year plan.

Under the plan, growth is linked to adequate public facilities. Unless all 11 public facility standards are satisfied within a zone, no development permit may be approved. The 11 facility standards are not just goals or guidelines, but rather precise performance standards.

MOTIVATING EMPLOYEES
TO IMPROVE PERFORMANCE

Motivation is often a function of measurement. Setting reasonable, measurable goals can create an expectation that those goals can be reached. Displaying progress toward goals, or just measuring present against past performance, often induces members of the workforce to work in positive directions; for example, taking pride in moving the trend lines in the "right" directions: more output, higher quality, more effective outcomes.

Saving and Improving. Florida state government has undertaken to institutionalize productivity improvement by identifying, implementing, measuring, and rewarding major cost savings and performance enhancements.

A public-private cooperative initiative, *Partners in Productivity,* was developed by two nonprofit organizations and supported by an explicit state government commitment. The program has three components: "report cards" identifying areas needing improvement, "scorecards" on how well objectives are being met; and "productivity awards" to recognize and reward success. In its first year (1990) cost saving and management improvement recommendations saved $99 million; a first-in-the-nation performance and productivity measurement system was incorporated into law and used as a yardstick for future funding of agencies; and in pursuit of better performance, employees have become engaged in total quality management methods. Evidence of cost savings was particularly important in building legislative and media support: Performance improvement without concomitant evidence of savings would not have been as politically salient.

Getting Citizen Feedback. The City of Paramount, California, has instituted a citizen *Law Enforcement Evaluation System* that has resulted in improved service accountability and service delivery, more productive community interaction, and reduced crime levels.

In 1982, the Rand Corporation published a Department of Housing and Urban Development (HUD)-sponsored study on conditions of U.S. suburbs of over 10,000 people. The city of Paramount ranked as one of the eight "most disastrous" American suburbs, scoring in the bottom in 9 of 16 disaster indicators, and ranking 31st in California in the category of number of serious crimes committed per 100,000 population. Gangs were rampant, graffiti was pervasive, and crime was increasing. Because of the cosmopolitan nature of the community, with its large Hispanic population, it was difficult for law enforcement to relate to the community, and the community was outraged at the poor service it was receiving.

Public perception of poor service delivery was exacerbated by the use of deputies from L.A. County. Because individual deputies might work in the city only 1 or 2 days per month on a rotational basis, they appeared apathetic as to the quality of service delivery.

To combat this situation, the city implemented several programs. To make sheriffs recognize that they were accountable to the city, specific officers were assigned to Paramount on a full-time basis. The city seal was affixed to officers' patrol cars. Most important, in order to create more accountability; to improve the quality of service delivery; and to provide more effective, efficient, and productive law enforcement service delivery, the city initiated the Law Enforcement Evaluation System. This program requires the deputies, upon completion of service, to hand out evaluation forms to every victim or complaining party after each call. All the resident has to do is put check marks in boxes and mail the preaddressed postcard to the sheriff's station in order to evaluate the city's law enforcement service.

Every 3 months, a recap of the data is provided to the City Council. Each deputy also receives a copy of every returned card evaluating his or her performance. Whenever a negative comment is received on an evaluation form, the lieutenant calls the citizen to resolve or respond to the complaint.

The results of the Citizen Satisfaction Survey Forms have provided important assessments of performance: 93% rated the deputy as courteous, while only 1% rated the deputy as indifferent. In 83% of the cases the deputy's performance was rated as excellent and in 13% of the cases the deputy's performance was rated as good. In only 1% the deputy's performance was rated as fair, and 3% rated the deputy as "other." Assuming that dissatisfied citizens were at least as likely to return the forms, the overall response pattern was decidedly positive, and the response rate of 20% exceeded the 1%-3% response that is typical of market research surveys.

Deputies previously thought that residents were hostile. Instead, they often found that they were actually appreciated. This has improved their attitude toward the community. Instead of hundreds of complaints and gripe sessions, there is now only an occasional complaint, along with productive Neighborhood Watch meetings and praise and understanding for deputies. Gang activity has decreased. The community feels that deputies are providing a higher quality of service in the context of more open communication with residents.

CONCLUSION

As the EXSL cases illustrate, managers who are responsible for day-to-day management (Hatry & Fisk, 1992) now often have access to information with which to implement public policy, and often use that data to improve services. Performance measurement is especially useful in the budgeting and fiscal area: estimating resource requirements, justifying budgets, reducing costs, reallocating resources, investing increased resources, and improving benefit-cost linkages.

Measurement-based best practices are becoming models for the entire public sector. Working from the premise that measurement of performance and of financial management are intertwined, the Government Accounting Standards Board (GASB) has stated that the goal of service delivery would be well served if debates about service allocation and resource utilization were guided by objective criteria (Fountain, 1997). GASB has made major progress toward the development and widespread use of objective measures in municipal budgets and fiscal reports. The impetus for this effort has been widespread concern that lack of such data undercuts the efforts of government to communicate information about its efficiency and effectiveness; that the financial reports of governmental entities do not go far enough in providing "complete information to management, elected officials and the public about the 'results of the operations' of the entity or its programs" (Fountain, 1992, p. 1). The National Center for Public Productivity (1997) and other organizations are, in conjunction with the Sloan Foundation, now establishing pilot projects that provide a results-oriented, citizen-driven basis for performance improvement in the public sector.

REFERENCES

Ammons, D. N. (1996). *Municipal benchmarks: Assessing local performance and establishing community standards.* Thousand Oaks, CA: Sage.

Fountain, J. (Ed.). (1992). *Service effort and accomplishment project* (1st ed.). Norwalk, CT: Government Accounting Standards Board.

Fountain, J. (Ed.). (1997). *Service effort and accomplishment project* (2nd ed.). Norwalk, CT: Government Accounting Standards Board.

Government Accomplishment and Accountability Task Force of the American Society for Public Administration. (1996). *Performance measurement training.* Washington, DC: Author.

Hatry, H. P. (1978). The status of productivity measurement in the public sector. *Public Administration Review, 38,* 28-33.

Hatry, H. P., & Fisk, D. M. (1992). Measuring productivity in the public sector. In M. Holzer (Ed.), *Public productivity handbook* (pp. 139-160). New York: Marcel Dekker.

National Center for Public Productivity. (1997). Results-Oriented, Citizen-Driven Performance Measurement Project, Rutgers University, Newark, N.J.

7

COMPREHENSIVE IMPROVEMENT

──■

Integrated Approach

Management For Quality ─┐
Development of Human Resources ─┤
Adapting Technologies ─┤
Promoting Partnerships ─┤
Performance Measurement and Evaluation ─┘

MULTIPLE OPPORTUNITIES FOR IMPROVEMENT
■──

Although the EXSL cases in the preceding chapters are grouped by major improvement factors, cases of exemplary progress often result from multiple approaches to the improvement of public performance integrating several of the major approaches detailed in the preceeding chapters (Figure 7.1.). The advantages of a multi-dimensional approach are also confirmed by other-than-EXSL cases, for example:

■ The impressive turnaround of the New York City Department of Sanitation was shown to result from technological innovation, labor-management cooperation, and improved measurement practices.

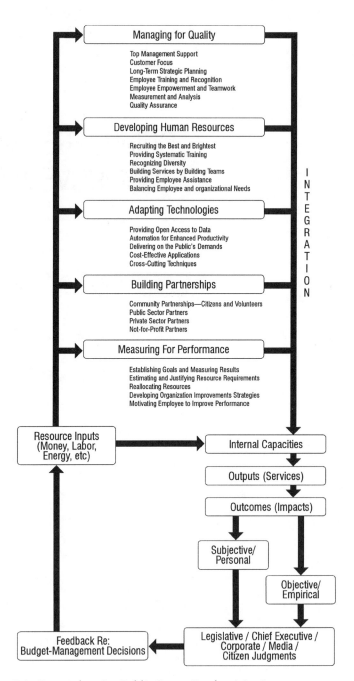

Figure 7.1. Comprehensive Public Sector Productivity Improvement

■ Performance improvement at the Jacksonville Electric Authority was the result of successful financial strategies, strong leadership, and keen understanding of the organization's culture.

■ Revitalization of the Pennsylvania Department of Transportation was possible due, among other things, to securing political support, enhancing management capacities, and strategic development of the organization.

■ A performance turnaround at the Village Creek Wastewater Treatment Plant in Fort Worth, Texas, emphasized three aspects of organizational change: the larger external environment, technology, and internal personnel dynamics.

Although each such comprehensive approach required a major commitment of political will and real resources, the investment was less a gamble than a sure bet; one lesson of EXSL and other models is that integrated improvement programs have an advantage: Investments suggested by managerial analysis, citizen survey, or employee input can be followed by necessary investments in information, technology, or training.

Public sector improvement programs operate under many labels. The program's name, however, is less important than its substance: comprehensive productivity improvement in an environment of increasing demands and reduced resources. Such programs improve performance systematically, by integrating advanced management techniques and, in the best cases, institutionalizing productivity improvement initiatives. Some EXSL cases offer such comprehensive models. Some examples follow.

Managing Productively. In the late 1980s, Hillsborough County, Florida, confronted an accelerated rate of growth; on average, 20,000 people a year were moving into the county. Such rapid growth led to increased demands for county services, which in turn posed new problems. The provision of quality services to all residents, new and old, was complicated not only by the growth in population, but also by a lack of continuity in leadership. The position of county administrator had been "turning over" every 2 years, straining relationships with both the Board of County Commissioners and county employees. Top administrators in the county, as well as members of the Board of County Commissioners, agreed that dramatic organizational changes would have to be made in order to "provide quality public service second to none." The overall goal of the newly established *Operations Improvement and Development Department* was to enhance public service delivery, reduce the cost of public service, and improve the quality of services to the residents of the county.

The creation of the department was one of several changes that included the restructuring of the county organization to flatten the layers of decision making, and the creation of a new professional ladder in which compensation is based on performance. The department is staffed by a team of professionals who are experts in process consulting, organizational development, management development, strategic planning, and operations planning. It is part of the Productivity and Service Team, which includes Public Information, Cable Services, Information Technology, Legislative Liaison, and Human Resources. These departments share the common goal of improving overall productivity through such actions as the hiring and retaining of competent and committed staff and keeping up with the latest technology. This mission is accomplished through supporting and developing the following:

1. Employee involvement improvement teams
2. Work simplification teams
3. InterSolve teams
4. Management training
5. Employee and trade skills training
6. Strategic planning
7. Technology transfer

An overall emphasis has been on measurable results. Documented cost savings and cost avoidances totalled $3.59 million in the first year. Through 1995, documented cost savings and cost avoidances totalled more than $20 million. One indication of the success of the program is the broad spectrum of departments that have documented savings. The program works not only in those easily measured departments that have "hard" service savings, such as Solid Waste and Public Utilities but also in the "softer" delivery areas such as Social Services and Aging Services. Another indicator of the success of the program is found in the results of the Employee Survey. This survey measured employee satisfaction on a broad range of job components. The results indicated that employees who participate on employee teams or in training and development programs were more satisfied overall than those employees who did not participate in these programs.

Emphasizing Service. Despite cuts following voter approval of California's Proposition 13 in 1978, a comprehensive emphasis on management for quality has helped San Diego improve services through its *Service Enhancement Program.*

At the beginning, under the pressures of Proposition 13, the attitude of many employees at the City of San Diego reflected the resentment of having to increase their productivity without the resources—the personnel, training, equipment, and office space—they perceived as necessary to do their work.

The city manager wanted to change the attitude of employees at all levels of the organization, training them to act as "if our customers had a choice, they'd choose us." This motto and the City Mission Statement became the foundation for 1988—The Year of Service. In February of that year, the city manager's office requested proposals from all department directors for programs designed to enhance citywide services to customers, citizens, and employees. Three departments—Building Inspection, Parks and Recreation, and Fire—were selected to participate in the first phase of such a program. The experiment has been successful, and key components of a comprehensive program that has developed from that initiative include the following:

1. Development of performance measures to assist each department in monitoring the effectiveness of their service

2. Development and administration of pre and post citizen surveys

3. Development of a quarterly service-oriented employee newsletter

4. Citywide training in customer service philosophy and techniques

5. Inclusion of a customer service function and standards in each employee's performance evaluation

6. Revision of citywide policies and procedures to streamline them for service to the customer

7. The development of a telecommunications system to improve communication to city customers

Planning Productivity Improvement. The South Florida Water Management District (SFWMD) received an EXSL award for the *Water Management Productivity Improvement Program (PIP).* PIP is a comprehensive design that addresses widespread public demands for optimal utilization of scarce governmental resources. It enhances overall district performance, while at the same time encouraging widespread public commitment and support. Under PIP, productivity improvement is defined as a centralized effort to control the yield of resources put into a public agency. District resource expenditures are clearly linked to strategic initiatives based on current mission priorities.

The five main components of the district PIP are:

1. Department/program designed productivity plans
2. A productivity improvement advisory council
3. A districtwide steering committee
4. Departmental PIP task forces
5. A central coordinating unit

These components were established as a result of an exercise that integrates administrative structure with a management planning system. This is an activity that defines a holistic districtwide productivity improvement program in a continuous quality improvement environment. The program equates to an overall enhancement of the quality of work life at the district while improving quality of services in meeting public demands.

CREATING DETENTION ALTERNATIVES:
COOPERATION, NOT INCARCERATION

The productive potential inherent in multidimensional problem solving is also illustrated by multiple EXSL cases across one functional area: detention. Four EXSL cases illustrate the problem-solving synergy that can result from "breaking out" of traditional, bureaucratic patterns of thinking.

The McLean County (Illinois) *Extended Day Program (EDP)* is designed for the purpose of providing the county court system with an alternative to secure detention. Due to a change in judicial ordinances, which called for the removal of all juveniles from adult jails, McLean County lost the ability to detain minors locally. The county's options were to detain minors outside the county at a cost of $75.00 per day, or develop an alternative solution. The EDP was developed as a cost-saving option. The program is designed for the purpose of providing the county court system with an alternative to secure detention. The EDP targeted a specific population of minors, aged 11 to 17, who were involved with the juvenile justice system. The program allows minors who should be in secure custody an opportunity to remain in the community by providing the structure that a detention center provides, but in a nonsecure setting. Minors are offered the following services on a daily basis:

tutoring, group therapy, and basic life skills. Each minor must provide a service to the community.

The program produces swift consequences for violations of probation. Rather than wait for court hearings on the violations, with the probable outcome being some type of dispositional detention, the minor is immediately ordered into the program. The program further allows for minors who have been charged with a serious offense to be detained initially, but then allowed home confinement, with the restrictions that they attend the program on a daily basis.

The EDP, which was originally unique in the state of Illinois, is innovative in that it is an alternative to detention. It offers avenues other than detention for juvenile delinquents, although detention is often the easier option. This program permits juveniles to function in a very structured, but unlocked, setting and provides those minors with the community resources that are important for shaping and challenging youth. One of the positive outcomes of EDP is that minors do not mind being in the program. Many of the "graduates" drop by to see the staff or other providers. They typically view their service projects as a positive contribution to the community, not just something that an adult tells them "needs to be done." Minors have taken pride in the program and see themselves as being a "part" of it rather than just a "body."

With similar objectives, in the late 1970s the state of California moved to address the pressing needs of 17- to 21-year-old undereducated at-risk urban youth through a highly structured 6-week education and job preparation model, the *Innovative Military Programs and Civilian Training (IMPACT)* program. In particular, IMPACT is designed as an alternative to incarceration. In response to the problem of high youth unemployment, IMPACT's highly structured, short-term education and job-placement curriculum encompasses basic, premilitary, and preemployment skills. Training is provided by a combination of National Guard and civilian instructors who apply the military's highly disciplined approach to teaching/learning techniques, coupled with traditional education methods and philosophies. From 1977 to 1995, IMPACT enrolled 7,017 participants and successfully placed 5,405: 28% entered military service, 57% were employed, and 15% returned to accredited schools. The cost was approximately $1,900 per participant, compared to $25,000 per year for incarceration.

In 1983, in response to the prison overcrowding crisis of the late seventies, the state of New Jersey developed the *Intensive Supervision*

Program to prevent prison overcrowding and to improve the screening of nonviolent offenders who are eligible for early release into the community. It is a highly structured program encompassing electronic and substance abuse monitoring, full-time employment, community service, and repayment of court-ordered fines and penalties. By diverting hundreds of prisoners from the system, the high cost of building an additional correctional facility for more serious offenders was avoided.

The program involves intensive screening of inmates who are a minimal threat to the community. They are released into an extremely restrictive but supportive environment where they are monitored by staff and electronic surveillance, must comply with a curfew, maintain full-time employment, perform community service, satisfy financial obligations, and undergo substance abuse monitoring and counseling. In 1995, the cost of supervising an ISP participant was about $7,500, compared to estimates of $35,000 to incarcerate an offender. The program has achieved cumulative savings (i.e., cost avoidances) of approximately $70 million for the state.

In Durham County, North Carolina, the *STARR (Substance Treatment and Recidivism Reduction) Program* is a 12-step substance abuse treatment, life skills education, and community referral effort designed to keep a targeted inmate population (both male and female) in recovery and out of jail. During the 4-week program, 20 local agencies/groups work directly with the STARR Program inmates.

There are four components of the STARR Program, encompassing a minimum of 75 hours of class/group time required of all inmate graduates:

1. Substance abuse lectures/recovery therapy groups
2. Self-help classes/community referral enrollments
3. Life skills education/12-step meetings
4. Continuing care management/tracking

The STARR Program was implemented not as just another in-jail substance abuse treatment program, but as a comprehensive quality-improvement program that also addresses inmate issues of financial, social, medical, legal, housing, family, educational, and recovery needs. It was initially funded by a grant from the Governor's Crime Commission as a model program for the state of North Carolina. Since October 1990, more than 1,000 inmates have entered and more than 800 have graduated from STARR, with a graduate rearrest recidivism rate of only 29%

(thus saving Durham County government just over $150,000 in inmate jail time/expense).

HOUSING: IMPROVING TENANTS' LIVES

Decent, affordable housing is a priority for our society, and the two EXSL programs below serve the housing needs of low- and moderate-income clients. Because they are comprehensive approaches—applying a range of support services rather than focusing narrowly on building management—they measurably improve the quality of tenants' lives.

A New Lease on Life, a program of the State of Colorado, focuses on the ambitious outcome of enhancing clients' quality of life rather than the more limited, but more easily achieved, workload measures such as tenant occupancy.

In keeping with the movement toward deinstitutionalizing the mentally disabled, the Colorado Department of Institutions established this program in 1977—long before *quality* was a buzzword in either the public or private sector—specifically to meet the public housing needs of persons with mental disabilities. This program has been successful on two dimensions: It offers alternatives to institutional living, and it rehabilitates existing housing stock.

A New Lease on Life, in conjunction with subsidies from the federal Department of Housing and Urban Development, provides housing assistance for more than 1,200 disabled persons. Before receiving this assistance, most tenants resided in substandard housing units, were homeless, or were institutionalized. Under the program, the tenant pays approximately 30% of his or her income toward rent, with the average client paying around $96 dollars per month for a $325 per month apartment. Unlike other housing programs, this program offers support services to the client, including case management, mental health counseling, and job training and skills development. Program coordinators, who are specifically trained to evaluate the participants, monitor the services provided to the client population. The direct impact of the program can be measured in terms of the quality-of-life enhancements realized by the clients served: They are afforded clean housing and myriad support mechanisms, as well as the opportunity to live as independently as possible.

A New Lease on Life relies heavily on the cooperation of a number of state and local agencies whose combined resources enable the program to offer decent, affordable housing to mentally disabled individuals. The program has been at the forefront of recognizing the linkage between support services and housing, which ultimately helps the client to become more self-sufficient. This "bootstrap" approach has now become part of the federal government's effort to supply housing to the mentally disabled. The program also facilitates an individual's integration into the community, which stresses the importance of access to basic community-based and real-world services such as banks, churches, shops, and mental health support agencies.

Operation Hand Up was inaugurated in 1992 by the City and County of Honolulu to offer a helping hand to employable individuals by giving them clean, subsistent housing, laundry and shower facilities, and one hot meal a day for $200 a month; four options for work or job training; and counseling for drug or alcohol abuse, stress management, and other personal problems. The program is designed not to be a handout, but a hand up to independence and regained self-esteem.

To implement the pilot program, the city leased warehouse space from the state of Hawaii and converted it into 39 individual cubicles, plus space for an office, a kitchen, laundry facilities, and men's and women's bathrooms and showers. The cost of materials to erect the Operation Hand Up facility, named Hale Kai (Sea House), was funded by the City and County of Honolulu Building Department. The annual budget is funded by the city's Department of Housing and Community Development.

MULTIPLE SOURCES OF COOPERATION

Three EXSL cases illustrate the need for many sources of cooperation in departing from traditional hierarchical arrangements:

Raising Expectations. River of Dreams is the first National Park Service-sanctioned Grand Canyon raft program for people with significant physical, medical, and mental disabilities. The City of Phoenix Parks, Recreation and Library Department collaborated with nonprofit organizations and commercial outfitters to pioneer this landmark program of accessibility. In the fall of 1991, the City sponsored the first National Park Service-sanctioned Grand Canyon raft trips for people facing significant physical disabilities and life-threatening illnesses. Two trips were offered, each spanning 2 weeks and 225 river miles through some of the highest-rated whitewater rapids in the country. Most of the participants had never before rafted or camped out-of-doors. Their backgrounds were diverse, but all shared a life-long desire to experience the Grand Canyon firsthand rather than through someone else's words. This program has shown that the nation's natural environment is everyone's birthright, and that some of the country's most inaccessible terrain can be safely accessed through creative thinking, hard work, and open attitudes.

Cooperating via Committee. In Seattle, recognizing the increasing number of incarcerated persons who suffer from mental illness, the Kings County Department of Adult Detention established the *Kings County Correctional Facility Mental Health Committee* program, which addresses the different needs of mentally ill offenders in public prisons.

Working to better understand and satisfy the special needs of such offenders in county jails, the Correctional Department joined forces with the Department of Human Resources to form the Mental Health Committee. It is charged with enhancing the availability of mental health services to prisoners while incarcerated and upon their release. The committee is also involved in generating greater community involvement in addressing the problem of mentally ill offenders. By increasing public awareness and developing strategies to bring appropriate services to the community, the program relies heavily on existing resources and expertise and is therefore cost-effective.

The committee has brought together mental health advocates, judicial representatives, police, and corrections and clinical experts to analyze the growing mental health problem among the correctional population, and to propose workable, coordinated solutions. Specifically, the program has improved the quality of life of mentally ill offenders by establishing support mechanisms, by de-emphasizing the punitive nature of incarceration, and by promising the offender continuation of care upon release from a county prison. It has increased the number of intensive community treatment care centers in King County, and has more than doubled the number of mentally ill offenders served. It offers a model for other municipalities with regard to cooperative efforts among agencies and the ability to put forth solutions to the growing problem of mentally ill offenders in a timely and cost-effective manner.

A STEP-BY-STEP STRATEGY

Complementing the improvement factors of Figure 7.1, public sector performance improvement programs typically follow a multiple-step strategy (Holzer, 1995):

Step 1. Clarifying Goals and Obtaining Support. Productivity programs must agree upon, and have commitments to, reasonable goals and objectives, adequate staff and resource support, and organizational visibility. The full cooperation of top management and elected officials is a prerequisite to success.

Step 2. Locating Models. Because productivity is an increasing priority of government, existing projects can suggest both successful paths and ways to avoid potential mistakes. Models are available from computer networks, the professional literature, and at conferences.

Step 3. Identifying Promising Areas. As a means of building a successful track record, new productivity programs might select as targets those functions continually faced with large backlogs, slipping deadlines, high turnover, or many complaints. Because personnel costs are the largest expenditure for most public agencies, improved morale, training, or working conditions might offer a high payoff. Organizations might also target functions in which new techniques, procedures, or emerging technologies seem to offer promising paybacks.

Step 4. Building a Team. Productivity programs are much more likely to succeed as bottom-up, rather than top-down or externally directed, entities. Productivity project teams should include middle management, supervisors, employees, and union representatives. They might also include consultants, clients, and representatives of advocacy groups. If employees are involved in looking for opportunities, then they are likely to suggest which barriers or obstacles need to be overcome; what tasks can be done more efficiently, dropped, or simplified; which workloads are unrealistically high or low.

Step 5. Planning the Project. Team members should agree on a specific statement of scope, objectives, tasks, responsibilities, and time frames. This agreement should be detailed as a project management plan, which should then be updated and discussed on a regular basis.

Step 6. Collecting Program Data. Potentially relevant information should be defined broadly and might include reviews of existing databases, interviews, budgets, and studies by consultants or client groups. A measurement system should be developed to collect data on a regular basis, and all data should be supplied to the team for regular analysis. The validity and usefulness of such information should be constantly monitored.

Step 7. Modifying Project Plans. Realistic decisions, based on continuing team discussions of alternative approaches and data, must be made about program problems, opportunities, modifications, and priorities. For instance, would a problem be solved best through the more intensive use of technology, improved training, better supervision, or improved incentives?

Step 8. Expecting Problems. Projects are more likely to succeed if they openly confront and then discuss potential misunderstandings, misconceptions, slippages, resource shortages, client and employee resistance, and so on. Any such problem, if unaddressed, can cause a project to fail.

Step 9. Implementing Improvement Actions. Implementation should be phased in on a modest basis and without great fanfare. Projects that are highly touted, but then do not deliver as expected, are more likely to embarrass top management (and political supporters), with predictable consequences. Projects that adopt a low profile are less likely to threaten key actors, especially middle management and labor.

Step 10. Evaluating and Publicizing Results. Measurable success, rather than vague claims, is important. Elected officials, the press, and citizen groups are more likely to accept claims of success if they are backed up by hard data. "Softer" feedback can then support such claims. Particularly important in providing evidence of progress are timely data that reflect cost savings, additional services, independent evaluations of service levels, client satisfaction, and reductions in waiting or processing times.

As with any other "generic recipe," this model should be modified and adapted to specific organizational contexts. Real cases will always be slightly different than the model; in some cases one or two steps might be missing because of the organizational and cultural assumptions of the situation; in other cases several steps can be combined into one. Still, because the steps of the model are analytically distinguishable, the model is useful for analyzing real organizations and programs to highlight the strengths and illuminate the weaknesses of cases under discussion.

CONCLUSION

Overall, then, the most innovative and productive public agencies do not simply execute one good program. Rather, they integrate advanced management techniques into a comprehensive approach to productivity improvement. They institutionalize productivity improvements by identifying, implementing, measuring, and rewarding major cost savings and performance enhancements in their agencies. They benchmark their efforts against similar organizations across the nation. They have a client orientation. Perhaps most important, productive programs are built on the dedication, imagination, teamwork, and diligence of public servants.

REFERENCE

Holzer, M. (1995). Building capacity for productivity improvement. In A. Halachmi & M. Holzer (Eds.), *Competent government: Theory and practice* (pp. 457-467). Burke, VA: Chatelaine.

8

AN EFFECTIVE
PUBLIC SECTOR

───■

■──

The cases presented in this volume are hard evidence that the public
sector does improve its performance. These entrepreneurial, innovative
programs are successes in stretching resources, in building problem-solving
capacities, and in helping to solve some of society's most difficult
problems. They are not unusual. Government quietly harbors thousands
of similar projects and has been accomplishing as much for decades.
Pressured public administration is continuing to improve in pragmatic,
productive terms. As Poister (1988) observes,

> despite the negative perceptions of the public bureaucracy that prevail in
> some quarters, successes are routinely scored by administrative agencies
> at all levels of government. These range from single episodes of satisfac-
> tory interactions with individual clients to the effective implementation
> of new programs and the development of innovative policies, strategies
> and treatments. (p. 27)

That record is counter to assumptions that public servants care little
about operational efficiency and effectiveness. Each program is the result

of work by motivated, dedicated individuals and teams, largely because professionals have taken the initiative to do so. As policy implementers who are on board for the long term, they are committed to improvement. They also understand that productivity improvement is not a technical, value-free impetus. For instance, government must "deliver" if it is to maintain its legitimacy. Failed projects fail to support the needs of democratic political institutions. Public servants are fully aware of this. Their commitments are at least as strong as those of transient (e.g., elected) policymakers, and their innovations are at least as promising and sophisticated as those proposed by their sometimes condescending corporate critics.

But the reality of "productive government" is considered an oxymoron by the public. In an era of prolonged retrenchment, in which the public service is suffering from a siege mentality, can anything reverse the image of an entrenched bureaucracy? Defensive pleas by those inside public organizations—that many public programs are underfunded and understaffed, that public management is better management than we might suspect—are not likely to excite those on the outside. To recruit allies, the public service must move toward a more innovative, less bureaucratic environment in which criticism is carefully considered rather than reflexively rationalized.

The problems of the late 1990s may be no greater than those that confronted us in the late 1960s, but the excitement and optimism that once attracted the "best and the brightest" despite chronic bureaucrat bashing—the confidence that public organizations are where the action is, that they can solve important societal problems—has been dissipated. In too many cases they have been replaced by a narrower vision of merely ameliorating or mitigating, rather than tackling, difficult problems.

Yet the problems that the public sector is asked to confront are as critical and compelling as ever: AIDS, homelessness, education, health care, environmental catastrophes. It is therefore essential to our society that public service be viewed as a compelling pursuit. We will have to look to public servants, as important links in the social system, to solve our most difficult problems. They are at the heart of the body politic's capacity to function, even survive, in increasingly stressful conditions.

Private initiatives alone are insufficient to solve society's collective problems, and are the cause of some: toxic pollution, dangerous products, unemployment in failing industries. Government must have the confidence of citizens. It must be the legitimate locus for solving society's problems through strategic plans and policies. It must have the capacity to be—not just promise to be—the vehicle for overcoming the sometimes narrow, self-centered, marketplace interests of profit-making organizations.

Private organizations also need government in order to produce private profits. Effective public services are, as always, a prerequisite to the private production of goods and services. The private sector is dependent not just upon defense but also a full range of *public* systems such as mass transit, education, vocational training, health care, criminal justice, sanitation, and postal services. The logic of that linkage is constantly reinforced by international organizations and corporations that are frustrated by government inefficiency in the developing world. A strong public sector is as important in their developed home country.

There are, however, two ironies. First, according to Eileen Siedman (1984), "the American public's love-hate relationship with its government produces demands for services, assistance, and protection while denigrating the people, processes, and costs necessary to meet those demands" (p. 4). Thus, playing to public opinion and the claims of privatization's proponents, many politicians have demeaned their own employees and virtually dismantled their own agencies. Second, the very people who struggle to respond to reduced resources suffer from lack of access to investments. Public employees could be even more productive if they had adequate funds to invest in adequate buildings, hardware, software, training, and more. Although "adequate" simply means approaching equity with the private sector, public agencies rarely have comparable funds for the investments that the private sector deems necessary to its own work. As compared to their private counterparts, public servants typically work in older buildings, with outmoded equipment and insufficient training.

Strengthening government's capacity to produce the services and outcomes we demand is not a simple undertaking. As Waldo suggests (Brown & Stillman, 1985), "Certainly some of what has been done and said in recent years seems to represent a belief that government is an enemy to be defeated, not an institution to be improved. . . . We should act to encourage creativity in public administration, but we haven't really addressed the matter seriously" (p. 460). And as Goodsell (1993) suggests, we need "a strategy of public action worthy of the public asset that is American bureaucracy" (p. 179). We need to establish a new, relatively nonbureaucratic environment in which personnel are rejuvenated rather than atrophied, managers are treated as professionals who are constantly in touch with new ideas, and the critiques of internal and external critics are sought out and taken seriously. In an environment of low confidence and low resources, a realistic agenda to accomplish those objectives must, in our opinion, include the three points discussed below.

1. *Have a positive impact on government's most expensive and extensive resources, its personnel.* We must make the best use of government's professionals as professional managers. We must enhance "regard and respect" for civil servants, thus encouraging recruitment and retention, and further building the capacity of career public servants to deliver public services as promised (*The Government's Managers,* 1987, p. 15). We (the authors) believe it is possible to overcome the low morale of a defensive public service, imaginatively recapturing the energy of the public service of the 1930s, 1940s, or 1960s. Our underlying premise is that a more dynamic, creative internal environment can improve government's capacities to attract the "best and brightest," to retain the most able professionals, to help reenergize excellent public servants who might otherwise burn out or bail out. That can happen despite the private sector's more appealing image, that "business is where the action is."

2. *Utilize low-cost or no-cost innovations.* Given the constraints of a very tight fiscal environment, it is particularly unrealistic to expect to raise compensation (i.e., salaries and performance bonuses) to competitive levels, although even the Grace Commission (1984) supported this point. Full pay comparability is prohibitive; we must take as a "given" that the private sector will continue to have advantages in higher pay and more extensive fringe benefits or "perks."

3. *Suggest new possibilities for change, moving beyond the base of existing innovations that are suggested in the literature and the best practices of award-winning projects.* The public service cannot afford to conduct the public's business "as usual." Management of the American corporate sector is restructuring itself in response to international competition. The Eastern European and former Soviet governments are attempting radical reformulation of themselves, politically and managerially. Under similar fiscal and ideological pressures, American public administration should reasonably be expected to respond to its own problems with a new realism. However, one important caveat is underscored by Ingraham, Romzek (1994) and others: Private sector models are not directly transferable to the public

sector. Although there is overlap in some processes and functions, the public sector operates from a basis of different, more complex values and priorities.

Drawing from the lessons learned from thousands of successes—programs recognized by EXSL and many other award programs—two recent reports are sophisticated blueprints for productive government.

A FEDERAL MODEL

In *Reinventing Government,* Osborne and Gaebler (1992) outline a cultural and behavioral shift in the management of government away from what they call a bureaucratic government toward an entrepreneurial government. To a large extent, *Reinventing Government* attempts to integrate the fair market/privatization literature (Savas, 1974, 1987, 1992) with the "excellence in management" literature (Peters & Waterman, 1982). According to Osborne and Gaebler,

> most entrepreneurial governments . . . empower citizens by pushing control out of the bureaucracy, into the community. They measure the performance of their agencies, focusing not on inputs, but on *outcomes.* They are driven by their goals—their *missions*—not by their rules and regulations. They redefine their clients as *customers.* . . . They *prevent* problems before they emerge, rather than simply offering services afterward. . . . They *decentralize* authority, embracing participatory management. . . . They prefer *market* mechanisms to bureaucratic mechanisms. (pp. 20-21)

Osborne and Gaebler's entrepreneurial model is characterized by strong interpersonal skills and a nurtured knowledge and discipline. *Reinventing's* principles devolve management responsibility to the lowest employee level. At the same time, the model advocates accountability to citizens and taxpayers (who are seen as consumers). It is this commitment to both the workforce and the taxpayer that makes *Reinventing Government's* organizational and management structure highly pluralistic in nature.

Following Osborne and Gaebler, reinvention was adopted as the overall theme of Vice President Albert Gore's National Performance Review (NPR) of the federal government in 1993. *The Gore Report on Reinventing Government* (Gore, 1993) has substantial implications for the public service. Although the NPR model is drawn from the federal experience, it is validated by, and shares many elements with, the EXSL-based model put forth in this book. Gore (1993) proposes to empower employees to get results through a four-step process:

Step 1: Cutting Red Tape
   Streamlining the budget process
   Decentralizing personnel policy
   Streamlining procurement
   Reorienting the Inspectors General
   Eliminating regulatory overkill
   Empowering state and local governments

Step 2: Putting Customers First
   Giving customers a voice and a choice
   Making service organizations compete
   Creating market dynamics
   Using market mechanisms to solve problems

Step 3: Empowering Employees to Get Results
   Decentralizing decision-making power
   Holding all federal employees accountable for results
   Giving federal workers the tools they need to do their jobs
   Enhancing the quality of work life
   Forming a labor-management partnership
   Exerting leadership

Step 4: Cutting Back to Basics
   Eliminating what we do not need
   Collecting more
   Investing in greater productivity
   Reengineering programs to cut costs

In our opinion, Step 3, Empowering Employees, represents the core investment under the reinvention rubric. That is, performance improvement is, at the foundation level, contingent on six actions:

Action 1. Decentralizing Decision-Making Power. A key part of this first step is doubling the average span of a manager's control. Gore's (1993) rationale for such a severe move is that it is both necessary and productive:

> Some employees may view such pruning as threatening—to their jobs or their chances for promotion. It is true that the size of the federal workforce will decrease. But our goal is to make jobs meaningful and

challenging. Removing a layer of oversight that adds no value to customers does more than save money: It demonstrates trust in our workers. It offers employees in dead-end or deadly dull jobs a chance to use all their abilities. It makes the federal government a better place to work—which will in turn make federal workers more productive. As private companies [and public agencies] have found, the key to improving service while redeploying staff and resources is thinking about the organization's staffing and operating needs from the perspective of customer needs. What does each person's task add in value to the customer? (p. 71)

Action 2. Holding All Federal Employees Accountable for Results. Gore (1993) quotes Senator William V. Roth, Jr.:

> If government is to become customer-oriented, then managers closest to the citizens must be empowered to act quickly. Why must every decision be signed-off on by so many people? If program managers were instead held accountable for the results they achieve, they could be given more authority to be innovative and responsive. (p. 74)

In proposing that all agencies begin developing and using measurable objectives and reporting results, as well as clarifying federal program objectives and developing written performance agreements with department and agency heads, Gore (1993) concludes that

> ultimately, no one can generate results without knowing how the "bottom line" is defined. Without a performance target, managers manage blindly, employees have no guidance, policymakers don't know what's working, and customers have no idea where they may be served best. Informed consumers are the strongest enforcers of accountability in government. (p. 77)

Action 3. Giving Federal Workers the Tools They Need to Do Their Jobs. Gore's premise is that

> transforming our federal government to do better will mean recasting what people do as they work. They will turn from bosses into coaches, from directors into negotiators, from employees into thinkers and doers. Government has access to the same tools that have helped business make this transformation; it's just been slower to acquire and use them. We must change that. We must give workers the tools they need to get results—then make sure they use them. (p. 77)

Key recommendations are to provide adequate training (especially the flexibility to finance training needs), upgrade information technology training for all employees, and eliminate narrow restrictions on employee training to help develop a multiskilled workforce.

Action 4. Enhancing the Quality of Work Life. Although the Report acknowledges that the federal government is considered a desirable place to work, it advocates a forward-thinking approach to improving employee satisfaction with the objective of helping them focus on customer concerns rather than worrying about their own personal problems. Gore's team argues that

> the federal government would be smart to keep abreast of workplace trends. Our increasingly diverse workforce struggles to manage child care, elder care, family emergencies, and other personal commitments, while working conditions become ever more important. Recent studies suggest that our ability to recruit and retain the best employees—and motivate them to be productive—depends on our ability to create a satisfying work environment. . . . The federal government must ensure that, as we move toward improving performance and begin to rely on every worker for valuable ideas, we create a workplace culture in which employees are trusted to do their best. (1993, p. 84)

Recommended actions include expanded "family-friendly" workplace options such as dependent-care services; abolition of employee time sheets and time cards for the standard work week; and a presidential directive committing the administration to greater equal opportunity and diversity in the federal workforce.

Action 5. Forming a Labor-Management Partnership. Gore's premise here is twofold:

> Consistent with the quality push, federal employees want to participate in decisions that affect their work [and] we can only transform government if we transform the adversarial relationship that dominates federal union-management interaction into a partnership for reinvention and change. (1993, p. 87)

He recommends two actions: establishing labor-management partnership as an executive branch goal, and establishing a National Partnership

Council to help implement that goal and to propose statutory changes needs to make such partnerships a reality.

Action 6. Exerting Leadership. Finally, Gore's frustration is that

> despite the federal government's solid core of capable employees, it lacks effective leadership and management strategies. . . . The sweeping change in work culture that quality government promises won't happen by itself. Power won't decentralize of its own accord. It must be pushed and pulled out of the hands of the people who have wielded it for so long. It will be a struggle. (p. 88)

Gore (1993) recommends not only a presidential directive on quality, but two types of appointments: a chief operating officer for every department, and a President's Management Council "to lead the quality revolution and ensure the implementation of National Performance Review plans" (p. 89).

Under this mandate, Gore reports hundreds of detailed, pragmatic initiatives. Some were fully implemented quickly, including streamlined review processes and identification of high-risk/high-impact research applications. Others, such as "Just-in-Time" modular grants and limited electronic submissions, were undertaken as pilot experiments. After three years of "reinventing government," Gore (1996) reported, for example, that

- The Government had reduced its workforce by nearly 240,000.
- Superfluous layers of management had been cut, eliminating nearly 54,000 supervisors.
- The Social Security Administration was rated first in an independent survey of the country's best 1-800 telephone services (public and private).
- The Internet was being utilized to allow citizen to do government business from their computers, such as obtaining business advice, downloading IRS forms, or filling out Small Business Administration loan forms.
- The Department of Agriculture dropped three million pages of government forms.
- The regulatory and administrative burden of government on citizens and businesses had been slashed by nearly $28 billion a year.
- More than 100 federal-local partnerships had been created to focus on the needs of individual communities.

A STATE AND LOCAL MODEL

■

At the state and local level, the Winter Commission Report on the state and local public service defines a complementary agenda that would impact positively on the public service by strengthening executive authority and flattening the bureaucracy. The Winter Commission is a 27-member group under the chairmanship of former Mississippi Governor William Winter. The members have been working diligently with some of the best talent this country has to offer to come up with solutions to performance obstacles in the public sector.

This Commission's findings reinforce EXSL's lessons. Removing the barriers to a high-performance workforce is viewed by the Winter Commission (1993) as a key step:

> The flat, lean agencies of tomorrow can only work if staffed by a new kind of employee. Public employees need the training to broaden their skills and horizons, and they need to be strongly encouraged to abandon the play-it-safe style of working in favor of taking risks . . . employees need to know that their opinion and judgment count. . . . Rather than seeing them as "personnel" to be micromanaged, managers prepared to make the commitment to the trust and lead approach to managing would benefit greatly by recognizing them as problem solvers and innovators— as a source of institutional savvy about what works and what does not. Instead of being placed at the bottom of every organizational chart, they should be elevated to the front line. As part of their new role, public employees need the freedom to take risks and to act quickly to solve problems themselves, even if that means they may make some mistakes. (p. 39)

According to Elizabeth Hollender of the Commission (Callahan, Holzer, & DeIorio, 1995),

> *Hard Truths/Tough Choices* is a great title, but this is a reality about state and local government now. We have to "shape up or ship out." There is no question about it. There is no longer any tolerance for sloppiness. The central idea in the Winter Commission report is that the way we need to do that is to move from "command and control" to what they nicely call "trust and lead." Now what does this mean? It means giving executives the room to change, and holding them accountable for what you get. It means creating lean and responsive bureaucracies, scraping away the barnacles of the civil service system which we have added on top of union agreements. It means eliminating layers of managers who are watching

each other to see what happens. It means getting personnel and budget and procurement agencies to serve the agencies that are there to do the work, rather than creating their own paperwork. (p. 11)

In particular, the Winter Commission (1993) recommends creating a "learning government" through five personnel-related actions:

1. Rebuilding Human Capital. "The Commission believes that states and localities should aim for a stable learning budget set at least three percent of total personnel costs" (p. 42).
2. Creating a New Skills Package. The Commission recommends that courses essential for performance should reflect a new set of competencies in team building, communication, and involving employees, and commitments to cultural awareness and quality.
3. Creating Financial Incentives for Learning. This would particularly utilize skill-based acquisition pay; that is, pay increases based on new skills.
4. Encouraging a New Type of Public Manager. Managers will have to relearn their jobs, with particular emphasis on their roles as coaches, benchmarkers, listeners, mentors, and champions.
5. Developing a New Style of Labor-Management Cooperation. Parallel to the Gore Report, the Winter Commission believes that an adversarial climate has predominated between labor and management, a climate that stifles innovation and feeds public cynicism. It concludes that management must move away from a command-and-control mentality by including workers in decision making at the start.

THE ETHIC OF PUBLIC SERVICE

Broad changes suggested by award-winning programs and the Gore and the Winter Commission Reports are necessary if government is to be perceived as the means to solving society's problems, rather than as another problem itself. But new ideas alone would be insufficient without committed, professional personnel.

What drives public sector innovation? The question is deceptively simple, but there is no simple answer. Rather, there are at least three competing premises: fiscal pressure, slack resources, and an ethic of public service.

1. *Fiscal Pressure*. One premise is that public sector innovation occurs only under fiscal pressure. This is the message of the cutback manage-

ment and privatization movement. The assumptions of those initiatives are that

- government is bloated, employing too many workers,
- a leaner public sector will be more efficient, somehow generating the same services with fewer employees,
- output to input ratios will improve as a smaller workforce (e.g., lesser inputs) produces services (e.g., same outputs) at the same quantitative and qualitative levels, and
- the loss of personnel will somehow be compensated for with better planning, management, automation, procedures simplification, and so on.

2. Slack Resources. A second premise is that innovation requires slack (or discretionary) resources. This is the model defined in the private sector literature with respect to innovative firms; that is, that profitable, productive change occurs only when "surplus" resources are made available to potential innovators.

3. Public Service Ethic. A third premise is that innovation occurs because public servants are highly motivated to respond to the needs of their clients.

We (Holzer & Olshfski, 1990-1996) have begun an empirical exploration of innovation through a survey and interviews of EXSL winners. We constructed, pretested, and revised a survey instrument that was sent to all national award winners (140), more than two thirds of which responded.

1. Did innovation occur in an environment of fiscal pressure?

EXSL winners were barely adequately funded. Only 32% judged themselves to have sufficient funding, and a further 5% claimed to be well funded. But a significant portion were somewhat strained (54%) or severely squeezed (9%). Thus, the availability of slack resources with which to innovate—the private sector model—is not evident here, with as few as 1 in 20 innovators having that potential. Rather, we might tentatively conclude that the majority of programs were under fiscal stress. But the existence of stress does not necessarily imply that innovation happened because of stress; it might have occurred despite that condition.

2. How did award-winning programs compare with other units of their department's budget?

Generally, EXSL programs were not perceived as favored, but were funded at about the same level as other programs under the broader organizational umbrella. Fully two thirds perceived themselves as neither better nor worse off than associated programs. Although 21% considered themselves better off, 12% of the innovators judged themselves as worse off. Thus, there is no clear evidence that they were favored organizationally.

3. How did EXSL recipients compare with their colleagues elsewhere?

When we asked EXSL winners to compare themselves to similar agencies in other districts or states, their responses were substantially different from intra-organizational comparisons. Many more judged themselves to be better off (39%) than worse off (5%). This difference may indicate that respondents operate in a relatively supportive environment for innovation. The percentage perceiving themselves as in the same position as their intra-organizational colleagues (56%) paralleled the perception of sameness vis-à-vis their extra-organizational contacts (67%).

Following these brief questions of differentiation, we then asked award winners to assess the importance of resources (tangible and intangible) and motivations. These rank orderings were intended to give us clues as to the important parts of a public sector innovation model, and the data do suggest some patterns.

4. Awardees were asked to rank order resources. That is, "How important were each of the following resources in allowing your group to pursue the innovation (Rank order, 1 = most important, 9 = least important)." The rankings by means appear as Table 8.1. Responses in Table 8.1 may indicate that support—external and internal—is considered the most important resource. This is confirmed by interviews with award winners:

> The key issue is how do you develop relevant support from different elected officials so it becomes easier for that elected official to say this is going to be tough, but let's do it.

> Our building is a city block long. I walk miles in there, lining up my support and promoting what I am doing.

If availability of funding is considered a manifestation of support, then the first five factors are all support oriented: top agency executives, committed personnel, political officials, funding, and client groups. But it is important to note that "having funds available" is only fourth

TABLE 8.1 Rank Orderings of Resource Factors Important to Innovation

Having support of top agency executives	2.41
Having committed personnel	2.54
Having support of political officials	3.76
Having funds available	4.22
Having support of client groups	5.22
Having flexible work content	5.81
Having a legal or judicial mandate	6.17
Having flexible time arrangements	6.32

on the list, suggesting that other factors are more important innovation "drivers."

Respondents also ranked possible motivations: "How important were the different motivations listed below to pursuing the innovation in your agency? (1 = most important, 9 = least important)." The rankings by means appear in Table 8.2. Note that rank orderings of motivations are much more clustered than in Table 8.1 (re: resources and support). This may indicate a more complex environment, with multiple factors at work in terms of motivation, whereas the important supportive elements were fewer in any one situation.

It is important to note that financial pressures—which could also be reflected as legal requirements (such as court orders) or elected officials' directives to cut back—are not perceived as particularly major factors. Although the third-ranked factor in Table 8.2 is "to save money," its distinction from the much lower factor of "to respond to budget cut-backs" may indicate that this group of innovators is self-motivated to be efficient, especially if we note that the fourth factor in importance is "to coordinate or eliminate duplication." The relatively minimal importance of external factors is also suggested by the low rankings attributed to "legal requirements" in Table 8.2 (9th of 9) and to the related "Having a legal or judicial mandate" in Table 8.1 (7th of 8).

Rather, innovative public servants may be primarily self-motivated. The public service ethic seems to be alive and well in the preeminence of "to do the right thing" (1st of 9) followed closely by "to respond to citizen demands" (2nd of 9). Thus, we might postulate that innovative public servants are responding to an abstract "calling." For example, interviewees frequently referred to intangible qualities that evoke commitment,

TABLE 8.2 Rank Orderings of Motivations Important to Innovation

To do the right thing	3.54
To respond to citizen demands	4.21
To save money	4.25
To coordinate or to eliminate duplication	5.37
To respond to agency executive directives	5.42
To reflect the interests and expertise of agency personnel	5.61
To respond to elected officials' directives	5.88
To respond to budget cutbacks	5.93
To meet a legal requirement	6.60

such as "leadership," "courage," "tenacity," "vision," and "passion." This is not the terminology of bureaucratic incrementalists.

PROFESSIONALISM AND PUBLIC SERVICE

To return to our initial list of premises, was fiscal pressure an external stimulus—forcing innovation in order to stretch resources? Adequate funding can neither be dismissed nor confirmed as a precondition for innovation. Although "having funds available" was not ranked as most important, it was 4th in the list of 8. A majority of the EXSL winners perceived themselves to have more financial support than did their colleagues in other districts or states. We might, however, question whether inadequate funding limited resources available for experimentation and innovation.

The weaknesses associated with funding factors may suggest that the management cutback and privatization proponents are on the wrong path. There are many opportunities to improve government services short of starving the "beast." In fact, government is not a menagerie of overfed, lethargic bureaucrats, but a highly trained cadre of committed professionals. Productive public service is about more than innovation and commitment. It is also about professional competence. And as compared to the private sector, government is much more professionalized. Civil servants are more often educated, trained, or certified as formal preparation for their responsibilities. Furthermore, they are often competitively selected through rigorous examinations, a process of objective selection that is much less common in the corporate world. Approximately 40% of all professional and technical workers are employed in the public sector, although less than 20% of the American workforce is on public payrolls. According to Mosher (1988), "more than one third (36.7%) of all government employees were engaged in professional or technical pursuits, more than three times the comparable proportion in the private sector (10.9%)" (p. 183); outside of education, the government:business ratio of professional and technical personnel is nearly two to one, 21.2% to 11.6% (Mosher, 1988, p. 183).

Many public servants also have substantial professional preparation for their public *management* responsibilities. More than 250 graduate programs offer the degree of Master of Public Administration (M.P.A.) under the auspices of the National Association of Schools of Public Administration and Affairs (NASPAA). Because effective management of government requires an appreciation of the particular missions, environment, decision-making patterns, and constraints of public sector organizations, the M.P.A. provides a core of competencies, known as the NASPAA Standards for Professional Master's Degree Programs in Public Affairs and Administration (NASPAA, 1992). According to NASPAA, the typical M.P.A. curriculum includes coursework in

- The management of public and, as appropriate, third sector organizations, including
  human resources
  budgeting and financial processes
  information, including computer literacy and applications
- The application of quantitative and qualitative techniques of analysis in policy and program formulation, implementation and evaluation, decision making and problem solving
- An understanding of the public policy and organizational environment, including
  political and legal institutions and processes
  economic and social institutions and processes
  organization and management concepts and behavior

Public sector executives may also hold the Master of Public Policy (MPP) degree, which is offered by more than 100 members of the Association for Public Policy Analysis and Management. Other credentials that are primarily relevant to the public sector are such degrees as Master of Public Health (MPH), Master of Criminal Justice (MCJ), and

Master of Social Work (MSW), each of which is offered by hundreds of institutions. Government employees also earn degrees in such fields as law, medicine, computer and hard sciences, engineering, and agriculture. Many hold more than one advanced degree.

Our survey also suggests that, in contrast to more straightforward models of innovation in the private sector (e.g., slack as a prerequisite), the public sector is a harder-to-manage environment that demands mastery of greater complexity. Balk (1992), for example, cautions that private sector theories are inadequate to the government context. An M.B.A., for example, does not usually deal with the political context and particular problems of a public sector environment; EXSL awardees clearly understand that ignoring "irrational" political values and processes can doom a public sector program. Coursey and Rainey (1991) also argue that the public sector context has important implications for behavior, process, and performance in public organizations. Moe and Gilmour (1995) believe that private sector techniques are often in conflict with the constitutional values of the public sector. Kingsley and Reed (1991) show that the public organizational context may be a more important factor than generic models of strategic decision process indicate, that context and managerial level influence perceptions of decision processes. Furthermore, the job of running an organization is often simpler in the private sector: Corporations can buy machinery/equipment without bidding; firms can hire without having their selection criteria automatically challenged in court.

The ethic of public service, implemented by competent public professionals, seems to be a strong thread in successful innovation by EXSL awardees, but it is not a sufficient strand. Table 8.1 underscores the need for support—internal and external—in the process of launching and maintaining an innovation. The three highest-ranking resources are all loci of support: top agency executives, committed personnel, and political officials. Table 8.2 complements this finding through the low rankings accorded external pressures such as elected officials' directives, budget cutbacks, and legal requirements.

The substantial research and experience with public sector productivity programs in scores of federal, state, and municipal agencies is sufficient to dispel misconceptions that executives care little about operational efficiency and effectiveness. It is true that some managers have given up trying to improve productivity or have given in to low expectations. But a more comprehensive view indicates that, as policy implementers who are on board for the long term, many managers and executives are professionally committed to productivity improvement. Their commitments are at least as strong as those of transient policymakers, and their innovations are at least as promising and sophisticated as those proposed by their sometimes condescending corporate critics.

Overall, then, we might conclude that—in an era of semi-permanent fiscal stress—commitment, professionalism, and intangible support are relatively more important than fiscal resources, either as budgetary pressures or as slack resources. This is an optimistic situation, for intangible resources such as professionalism and commitment and support are easier to generate and tap than are finite, limited dollars.

This argument can lead to further hypotheses. Despite budget cuts and limited resources,

- if public servants are treated as committed professionals who want to do the right things
- if internal innovators consciously seek to build support within the agency, the broader organization, and the political-client environment
- if public administrators receive enlightened political support
- if they are treated as administrative professionals on a par with their private sector colleagues, and
- if they are allowed to become less bureaucratic:

then:

- more productive innovations will be developed and implemented.

THE FUTURE OF THE PUBLIC SERVICE

EXSL and other "best practice" awards are particularly important because it has never been clearer that government is under pressure—not just to be productive or efficient and effective in the most straightforward meaning of the term—but to pull back from a broad range of public responsibilities—to privatize such basic functions as education, police, corrections, sanitation, airports, information systems, and more.

Our society is at a critical juncture. The public is losing patience with what it perceives to be unproductive government. Two roads seems to diverge. Under the broad banner of "privatization," one seemingly straight and sunlit road is a set of optimistic promises, defined by the argument that the private sector can deliver necessary public services not only more effectively, but even at lower cost. The myth is that government is neither businesslike nor adaptive.

The other road, perhaps winding and not as well illuminated, is composed of pragmatic responses to the weakening of public support—a set of solutions proposed by the public service to improve services to the public. The reality of productive government—which our award-winning programs illustrate—is distinctly different from the myth. There are some bureaucratic horror stories—just as there are in private sector bureaucracies. But beneath the surface of the stereotypes are many dedicated public servants and many hard decisions quietly made to save money, stretch resources, reorder priorities, invent and innovate. Government is often businesslike, does often tap all types of expertise, and can often deliver as promised. The EXSL awards are hard evidence that government works. They are the public sector parallels to the private sector's best practices—such as the Baldridge Award. In this era of skepticism about government, these awards are especially important.

To the extent the first path is chosen, the public service will be smaller, weaker, and a less enticing career choice. To the extent the public is convinced that by way of the second option the public sector can deliver services, efficiently and effectively as promised, then the public service will become a more promising career path.

Is there then a future for the public service in an era of privatization? The answer is likely to be "yes," under several optimistic scenarios as the record of public sector successes helps to rebuild public support:

1. *The privatization highway becomes a dead end as reality sets in.* Contractors do not deliver as promised, costs to the public rise quickly, and wages drop precipitously. As a "quick fix," privatization fades, although contracting remains an option for creative, productive public decision makers.

2. *Government competes successfully with the private sector.* Competition has been sold to the public and policymakers as the primary means to achieving efficiency. But only one form of competition—privatization (or private vs. private)—has been assumed. Competition can certainly improve organizational performance, but in linking competition to privatization the former concept has been defined too narrowly. We ought to consider "government as competitor" as an expanded set of approaches to the

problem of public productivity. The award-winning individuals and programs cited above are evidence that government is competent and can
compete.

3. *Internal competition within government is adopted as the best of both
worlds.* Recognizing the importance of public control of public services,
competition without privatization becomes an acknowledged alternative.
Agencies or units of government compete to provide services that are
appropriate only to public sector delivery systems.

Evidence from public sector productivity and innovation programs in
scores of federal, state, and municipal agencies should begin to dispel
misconceptions that executives care little about operational efficiency
and effectiveness. But a more sophisticated view indicates that, as policy
implementers who are on board for the long term, many managers and
executives are professionally committed to performance improvement.
Their commitments are at least as strong as those of transient policymakers, and their innovations are at least as promising and sophisticated as
those proposed by their sometimes condescending corporate critics.

If public servants are treated as administrative professionals on a par
with their private sector colleagues, and if they are allowed to become
less bureaucratic as suggested by the Gore and the Winter Commission
Reports, then more innovative programs and initiatives will be developed
and implemented. Public servants will act more as creative entrepreneurs,
less as bureaucratic civil servants. And the public sector will, in the
public's perception, be more businesslike, more deserving of the public's
tax dollars.

A public sector that holds the public's confidence is very much within
our grasp. Hummel (1984) suggests that *bureaucrat,* with its negative
connotations, should be replaced by *public servant,* with more professional connotations. Of course, the public service can neither mandate
nor manipulate that change. But that substitution of terms, as evidenced
by common usage, should be the measure of our success in transforming
government. To the extent performance improves, so will image. To the
extent image changes, so will language. *Bureaucrat* will slowly give way
to *public servant. Bureaucracy* will slowly give way to *public service.* And
the public will feel confident in turning to its public organizations for
solutions to society's problems.

REFERENCES

Balk, W. (1992). Organization theories as instigators of public productivity improvement action. In M. Holzer (Ed.), *Public productivity handbook* (pp. 531-550). New York: Marcel Dekker.

Brown, B., & Stillman, R. J., II. (1985). A conversation with Dwight Waldo: A agenda for future reflections. *Public Administration Review, 45,* 459-467.

Callahan, K., Holzer, M., & DeIorio, J. (Eds.). (1995). *Reinventing New Jersey.* Burke, VA: Chatelaine.

Coursey, D., & Rainey, H. G. (Eds.). (1991). Organizational behavior and processes in the public sector. *Public Productivity and Management Review, 14*(4), 351-354.

Goodsell, C. (1993). *The case for bureaucracy* (2nd ed.). Chatham, NJ: Chatham House.

Gore, A. (1993). *The Gore report on reinventing government.* New York: Times Books, Random House.

Gore, A. (1996). *The best kept secrets in government.* Washington, DC: Government Printing Office.

Grace Commission. (1984). *President's private sector survey on cost control.* Washington, DC: Government Printing Office, January 15.

Holzer, M., & Olshfski, D. (1990-1996). *Innovation survey of EXSL award winners.* Previously unpublished papers presented at Regional and National Conferences of the American Society for Public Administration and the National Public Sector Productivity Improvement Conferences.

Hummel, R. (1984). *The bureaucratic experience.* New York: St. Martin's.

Ingraham, P. W., Romzek, B. S., & Associates. (Eds.). (1994). *New paradigms for government: Issues for the changing public service.* San Francisco: Jossey-Bass.

Kingsley, G. A., & Reed, P. N. (1991). Decision process models and organizational context: Level and sector make a difference. *Public Productivity and Management Review, 14*(4), 397-414.

Moe, R. C., & Gilmour, R. S. (1995). Rediscovering principles of public administration: The neglected foundation of public law. *Public Administration Review, 55*(2), 135-146.

Mosher, F. (1988). Professionalism. In R. Stillman (Ed.), *Public administration: Concepts and cases.* Boston: Houghton Mifflin.

NASPAA standards for professional master's degree programs in public affairs and administration. (1992). Washington, DC: National Association of Schools of Public Administration and Affairs.

Osborne, D., & Gaebler, T. (1992). *Reinventing government.* Reading, MA: Addison-Wesley.

Peters, T., & Waterman, R. (1982). *In search of excellence: Lessons from America's best run companies.* New York: Harper and Row.

Poister, T. H. (1988). Success stories in revitalizing public agencies. *Public Productivity Review, 11*(3), 27-28.

Savas, E. S. (1974). Municipal monopolies versus competition in delivering urban services. In W. D. Hawley & D. Rogers (Eds.), *Improving the quality of urban management* (Urban Affairs Annual Reviews, Vol. 8) (pp. 473-500). Beverly Hills, CA: Sage.

Savas, E. S. (1987). *Privatization: The key to better government.* Chatham, NJ: Chatham House.

Savas, E. S. (1992). Privatization and productivity. In M. Holzer (Ed.), *Public productivity handbook* (pp. 79-98). New York: Marcel Dekker.

Siedman, E. (1984, Summer). Of games and gains. *The Bureaucrat,* pp. 4-8.

The Government's Managers: Report of the Twentieth Century Fund Task Force on the Senior Executive Service. (1987). New York: Priority Press.

Winter Commission: National Commission on the State and Local Public Service. (1993). *Hard truths, tough choices: An agenda for state and local reform. The first report of the national commission on the state and local public service.* Albany, NY: Nelson A. Rockefeller Institute of Government.

APPENDIX:
AWARD-WINNING GOVERNMENT

———————————————————————————■

EXEMPLARY STATE AND LOCAL AWARD WINNERS
1989-1995
■————————————————————————————

For more information on these and other award winning programs contact:

National Center for Public Productivity
Rutgers University
Graduate Department of Public Administration
360 King Boulevard
Newark, New Jersey 07102

Or visit the Center's World Wide Web site at:

http://newark.rutgers.edu/~ncpp

Note: Program descriptions reflect the status of each program at the time the award was made, as indicated by the award-year designation.

Some award-winning programs represent innovations that have since been adopted widely within the public sector, but were relatively unique at the time of the award. Some programs may no longer be operating as described due to a range of possible factors, such as turnover in elected officials who supported a project or funding cutbacks beyond the control of the program or the unit of government.

■ **Adolescent Information Data Collection**
Somerset County, New Jersey (EXSL 1990)

In 1986, the Needs Assessment Subcommittee of the Somerset County Youth Services Commission began to explore the feasibility of developing a statistical database to develop profiles of troubled adolescents and to enable them to plan accurately for the services they may need in the future. The Adolescent Information Form was developed as a comprehensive data collection mechanism. This one-page client description document is used by 28 different agencies in Somerset County.

■ **Affordable Housing Through Master Planned Communities**
State of Hawaii (EXSL 1994)

The State of Hawaii Housing Finance and Development Corporation (HFDC) formed partnerships with private industry developers to create three socioeconomically integrated quality lifestyle communities in Hawaii's three highest population growth areas. These Master Planned Communities integrate a mix of for-sale single-family and multifamily homes, rental housing, neighborhood parks, schools, churches, day care centers, and commercial and retail areas in a cost-effective and cost-efficient design that is constructed with minimum financial impact on taxpayers.

■ **APERCU Training and Development Program**
City of Loveland, Colorado (EXSL 1989)

A cooperative effort between private and public employers, this program provides training and development opportunities that enhance employees' insight into and understanding of their jobs, skills, community, health, safety, and personal and professional development.

■ Automated Fingerprint Identification System
Western Identification Network, Inc. (EXSL 1992)

This partnership allows each of its members to conduct fingerprint searches against approximately 1.2 million records in the Automated Fingerprint Information System. The Western Identification Network, Inc., includes as members the states of Alaska, California, Idaho, Montana, Nevada, Oregon, Utah, Washington, and Wyoming, as well as the U.S. Postal Inspections Service, the U.S. Secret Service, and the U.S. Immigration and Naturalization Service.

■ Automated Juror Selection and Juror Tracking System
Clarke County, Athens, Georgia (EXSL 1989)

A computerized system tracks juror eligibility and provides: complete and accurate tracking of a juror's history; truly random and impartial selection of juries drawn; jury drawing and processing at any time; freeing juries from tampering and human error; and sharing of jury responsibilities by a representative population. The system has resulted in administrative efficiency and cost savings, and is particularly suitable for smaller governments.

■ Automated New Hire Program
State of Massachusetts (EXSL 1994)

The program matches "new hire" information with records of parents who owe child support and automatically sends out a notice to the new employer reinstating the wage assignment whenever it finds a match. If the computer finds that the employee also owes past due support, it automatically increases the wage assignment by 25% to recover that past due support as well.

■ Automated TB Surveillance System
State of California (EXSL 1994)

Responding to a TB outbreak in June 1992, the California Youth Authority (CYA) developed a computerized medical record system that documents and tracks patients exposed to active TB. The CYA used the existing statewide telecommunications network to connect all facilities to the medical system in an effort to control the spread of airborne TB in a population of 20,000.

■ **Brea Job Center for Day Workers**
City of Brea, California (EXSL 1991)

To provide an orderly, regulated, matching employment service between documented and undocumented Latino day workers and employers, and to decrease community conflict, the city council and city manager established a job center with a self-governance feature and local community involvement. Fifty-four percent (54%) of the workers are now employed on a daily basis; in 1991, 13,000 jobs were filled, including 300 permanent placements; multiethnic conflict between day workers and Anglo residents has been minimized, and better understanding has been promoted on both sides.

■ **Bulk Lien Sale Initiative**
Jersey City, New Jersey (EXSL 1994)

The initiative addressed the city's impending bankruptcy and subsequent state takeover. The city faced a $40 million deficit (in a $280 million municipal budget) that was created by an extremely low tax collection rate of 78%, just 3 points above the 75% collection rate that triggers state takeover of municipal finances.

■ **Bureau of Administrative Adjudication**
City of New Orleans, Louisiana (EXSL 1989)

This program is an alternative to criminal prosecution of individuals who fail to correct public health, housing, and environmental violations. Fines are levied against guilty parties and contractors are hired at owner's expense to correct violations. A fund generated with revenues collected rewards residents who report illegal dumping and littering.

■ **Business Development Reorganization and Strategic Plan**
City of Virginia Beach, Virginia (EXSL 1991)

To attract new businesses and investment to the city, the 20-year-old Department of Economic Development was revitalized by realigning staff for higher productivity, encouraging citizen participation in strategic

planning, and developing a unique city/university technology partnership. Twenty-four (24) new companies settled in the city and 17 existing
companies expanded. Over 1,500 new jobs were created and $34 million
was realized in new investment.

■ **California New Prison Construction Program
State of California (EXSL 1991)**

To overcome a severe overcrowding crisis, a Planning and Construction Division was created to design and build new prisons expeditiously
and in a fiscally prudent manner. Fast track construction technology,
division management of the capital outlay, and innovative designs have
relieved pressures caused by the 300% growth in inmate population since
1980, winning public support for bond acts and revenue bonds.

■ **Campaign to Save Our Children:
Teen Pregnancy Prevention Project
Richmond, Virginia (EXSL 1994)**

This project effectively initiated a highly visible media campaign to
keep the teenage pregnancy prevention and abstinence message in the
public eye. The well-organized education initiative served to enhance the
family-based knowledge of prevention and continues to provide support
to the family through the use of bus placards, newspaper informational
ads, the *Aftermath* comic book, T-shirts, and radio commercials that
include contests.

■ **Capital Strategies and Review System
New Castle County, Delaware (EXSL 1990)**

In an effort to evaluate ongoing capital projects, a capital strategies
and review system provides more timely and accurate planning and fiscal
information to management, legislators, and the general public. The
program provides a valuable quantitative tool for strategic/fiscal planning; for authorizing capital projects; and for maintaining a continuous
capital program cycle throughout the year.

■ Caring for Kids Neighborhood Day Care Home Project
City of Jacksonville, Florida (EXSL 1989)

This neighborhood day care home project is a collaborative effort to increase options for motivated welfare recipients. The program helps them attain permanent self-sufficiency by becoming licensed family day care home providers. This project addresses the issues of long-term unemployment and welfare dependency; inadequate job skills and educational training; and an inadequate supply of neighborhood home day care centers. Interested welfare recipients can become licensed family day care home providers, thus achieving economic self-sufficiency.

■ Carlsbad Growth Management Plan
City of Carlsbad, California (EXSL 1989)

This growth management plan is an effective approach to managing city growth by ensuring the adequacy of public facilities and services. The most unique features of the program are its use of public facility performance standards and its comprehensive, detail-oriented approach to facility planning and financing, with the goal of managing growth based on compliance with 11 facility-based performance standards.

■ Chesapeake Bay Technical and Financial Assistance Program
State of Virginia (EXSL 1991)

To maximize water quality protection of Chesapeake Bay, its tributaries, and other state waters mandated by legislation in 1988, a citizens' board with state staff support actively assists local governments to meet requirements through training, technology, grants, and consultation. Local governments are changing the way land is managed and developed; matching grants have funded positions providing land use planning and storm water engineering skills for the first time; technology has brought services to rural areas; public participation also enables residents to address community goals and issues for the first time.

■ Child Advocacy Center
Baltimore County, Maryland (EXSL 1990)

A highly specialized and interdisciplinary partnership of four public agencies is charged with facilitating the investigation, assessment, and prosecution of child sexual abuse cases. The program is considered highly innovative due to its integrative approach to managing the cases of sexually abused children. Through interagency cooperation, the child and family are subject to a less stressful experience and are not over-whelmed by the enormity of the child welfare system.

■ Child Support Enforcement Agency (CSEA)
Clermont County, Batavia, Ohio (EXSL 1992)

This program helps to strengthen families and reduce welfare depend-ency by placing the responsibility for supporting children where it belongs—on the parents. As a result of successful enforcement tech-niques, children can enjoy the standard of living that existed prior to the separation of their parents. Child support helps make it possible for children to grow in confidence and competence and to become healthy, productive, independent adults, often with a positive relationship with the absent parent.

■ City of Greenville Home Ownership Program
City of Greenville, South Carolina (EXSL 1989)

A public-private venture provides for construction of modestly priced homes for purchase by low-income citizens. The program combines Federal Community Development Funds and below-market financing through the South Carolina State Housing Authority to address the lack of quality housing in low-income areas. In 4 years the program produced 22 new homes in two different neighborhoods and made a significant contribution to neighborhood stabilization and revitalization.

■ City-Wide Service Request System
City of Syracuse, New York (EXSL 1989)

A computerized service request system channels complaints and re-quests for various services to a centralized telephone system, enabling the city to track the disposition of the service request. Calls are priori-tized according to seriousness and nature of complaint/request. The program led to significant cost savings, as well as measurable increases in quality effectiveness.

■ **Citywide Computer Productivity Forum and Investment Fund**
City of New York, New York (EXSL 1991)

Limited communication within and among the city's 40 separate agencies, each with its independent computer bureau, inhibited exchange of information and mutual problem solving. Identification and funding of useful computer-based projects led to formation of the Micro-Mini-computer Coordinating Council (M2C2), an organization of computer managers. The Citywide Productivity Forum sponsored by M2C2 is now a major event for the computer community of the city's government; exchange of ideas and applications is increasing productivity; a Technology Investment Fund conceived by M2C2, in a special account created by The Fund for the City of New York, is used to finance promising technology-based projects.

■ **Civil Delay Reduction Program**
County of San Diego Superior Court (EXSL 1990)

Designed to alleviate the backlog and reduce the delay of civil cases, this program is based upon the practice of early and continual judicial involvement to reduce the pending age and backlog of civil cases filed in the court. The practical realities of implementing these principles require tact, enhanced communication, and innovative behavior on the part of judges, court staff, and the local legal community. The program was successful in modifying state statutes, and once a modified system became operational, reductions in delays were realized.

■ **Community Intensive Supervision Project**
Allegheny County, Pennsylvania (EXSL 1991)

To reduce recidivism among male juvenile chronic offenders (ages 10-17), three neighborhood-based centers provide intensive programs of counseling, tutoring, recreation, substance abuse education, community service, and family projects. Offenders are monitored electronically and are randomly checked (urinalysis) for drugs and alcohol. For less than half the cost of institutional treatment, 179 youths have been diverted from institutional placements during an 18-month period.

■ **Community Service Partnership**
  Montgomery County, Maryland (EXSL 1990)

A joint public-private partnership promotes volunteerism and com-munity involvement, culminating in Community Service Day, an annual event that matches volunteers with the needs of the community. The program was founded to promote existing volunteer efforts as well as to identify and coordinate new volunteer services, and in doing so, encour-aged creative community service initiatives.

■ **Competition and Costing: Competitive Bidding**
  Indianapolis, Indiana (EXSL 1995)

By enabling city workers to compete fairly against private sector vendors, Indianapolis has reduced its budget by $10 million. The savings are reinvested in the city, allowing Indianapolis to put more police officers on the streets and invest in a $500 million infrastructure rebuild-ing program, the largest in city history, without raising taxes. The program emphasizes competition, innovation, and entrepreneurial thought among city employees, together with the adaptation of activity-based costing to the public sector.

■ **Competition With Privatization**
  Phoenix, Arizona (EXSL 1990)

The Department of Public Works utilizes a nontraditional approach to competing with private industry to enhance the competitive atmos-phere of the department, increase productivity, and reduce costs. This effort allows government services to compete with private industry on an equal footing, as no decision to contract out is made prior to the call for public bids. This program encourages participative management and cooperation between unions and the city, in a combined effort to provide the highest level of municipal service to the taxpayer, at the lowest possible cost.

■ **Comprehensive System of Maternal/Infant Services**
  San Joaquin County, California (EXSL 1991)

In response to the challenges posed by inadequate prenatal care, the San Joaquin County General Hospital developed comprehensive services with support from public and private agencies, volunteers, grants, and improved utilization of existing resources. Seven serious county barriers to care were eliminated; enrollment in all prenatal clinics doubled in 3 years; "no show" rates for clinic appointments dropped to less than 10%; birth weights of babies born to substance-abusing women increased; and a smaller number of toxicology screen positive babies were born.

■ **Computer Verification of Voting Records at the Polls**
City of Burton, Michigan (EXSL 1990)

This program was designed to prepare the public for voting by computer, which will soon replace manual voting and voter registration. This program involves the use of portable computers and customized software designed to verify registration data, direct voters to their appropriate districts, and streamline the process of updating and correcting voter information.

■ **Contractor Responsibility Program**
Commonwealth of Pennsylvania (EXSL 1991)

To prevent state agencies from doing business with firms that have violated laws or regulations, have poor performance records, engaged in wrongdoing, or failed to pay taxes, a computerized Contractor Responsibility Program was instituted in 1990. Tax delinquencies are being paid and payments are kept current; contracts with poor performers have been avoided; additional work for state agencies has been minimal, with benefits greater than expected; several independent state agencies have adopted the program.

■ **Criminal Justice Commission (CJC)**
Palm Beach County, Florida (EXSL 1994)

The CJC is an innovative method for assisting county commissioners to obtain better cooperation and coordination of efforts on the part of various criminal justice system components. The mission of the CJC (by ordinance) is to study all aspects of the criminal justice and crime prevention systems throughout the federal, state, county, municipal, and private agencies within Palm Beach County and to make recommendations to the Board of County Commissioners on policies and programs. The CJC task forces, committees, and councils representing over 200 representatives of criminal justice agencies and concerned citizens of Palm Beach County, identify priorities, assess alternatives, and recommend solutions to local problems.

■ **Datashare**
State of Utah (EXSL 1990)

This service provides direct computer access to all state business registrations and code filings through an on-line computer remote access service. The service makes information pertaining to business incorporated in Utah available to interested subscribers throughout the state. Datashare facilitates the efficient and timely exchange of information about incorporation, debt, credit status, and legal liabilities of Utah-based businesses.

■ **Dispute Resolution**
San Diego County, California (EXSL 1990)

As an alternative to civil court litigation, this program is designed to reduce the load on increasingly congested court calendars by avoiding the civil court system. Staffed by trained volunteers, it leads to the successful resolution of civil complaints, resulting in quicker, less costly outcomes to business issues, domestic problems, neighborhood disputes, and landlord/tenant disagreements. It combats increasingly congested court calendars.

■ **Diversity Commitment**
San Diego, California (EXSL 1992)

In a proactive effort to be responsive to the diversity within its workforce, as well as the communities it serves, the City of San Diego has undertaken an organizationwide change effort. The diversity commitment is a long-term, strategic plan that includes data gathering and discussion, ongoing education, problem solving, and changes in systemwide policies and procedures.

■ **Economic Development/Government Equity Program (ED/GE)**
   Montgomery County, Ohio (EXSL 1992)

During the 1980s, Montgomery County, Ohio, faced economic pressures and fiscal constraints similar to those that plagued other local
governments. To cope with these trends, the county developed the
Economic Development/Government Equity (ED/GE) Program. The program seeks to strengthen the regional economic base, promote rational
countywide growth, leverage other public and private development
funds, and foster interlocal government cooperation.

■ **Electronic Benefit System**
   Ramsey County, Minnesota (EXSL 1990)

This program enhances the delivery of public assistance benefits
through the existing network of automated teller machines (ATMs),
eliminating the need for thousands of paper transactions. Clients are able
to access their benefits through three ATM networks and thus do not
have to worry about benefits being lost or stolen. There is strong public
support for this system as the EBS is no costlier than the old method of
check issuance.

■ **Employee Assistance Program**
   City of Buena Park, California (EXSL 1989)

In a holistic approach to alleviating the personal problems of city
employees, the City of Buena Park provides in-house counseling in the
areas of stress, alcohol and drug abuse, family and marital crisis, job
problems, child and spousal abuse, and money and credit management
problems. Prior to EAP, the city psychologist worked in crisis intervention
with the city police department and there was no method to handle
general employee population problems. Most agencies this size traditionally contract out their EAP services; this program shows it can be done
in-house at considerable savings.

■ **Employee Assistance Program**
   City of Memphis, Tennessee (EXSL 1990)

In 1988, the City of Memphis established a broad-based assistance
program designed to address the various counseling, rehabilitation, and

crisis intervention needs of city employees. The city estimated it was losing $3,500,000 due to reduced efficiency, absenteeism, and accidents as a result of untreated disorders. The program has proven its cost-effectiveness based upon the estimate that for every dollar spent in EAP, four dollars are returned in reduced health care costs and improved efficiency and attendance.

■ **Enhanced Budget Presentation**
  City of Stamford, Connecticut (EXSL 1989)

An annual book of budget-related information was developed to provide explanatory back-up to the 200+ pages of computer printed tables that had traditionally been the budget decision tool. This volume proves invaluable to the fiscal boards as they make their budget decisions, as it enhances the original computer printout. This book describes the mission of each department, selected operating statistics, and a 10-year history of department revenue and expenditures.

■ **Environmentally Sensitive Lands Acquisition Program**
  Palm Beach County, Florida (EXSL 1994)

The program was developed in response to citizen concerns that environmentally sensitive lands in the county were rapidly being lost to development. These lands contain native plant communities, wildlife populations, endangered plant and animal species, and water recharge areas. The voters of Palm Beach County passed a $100 million bond issue to fund the acquisition of approximately 25,000 acres of environmentally sensitive lands. The county formed a partnership with The Nature Conservancy to provide a variety of services related to the management of these lands.

■ **Extended Day Program (EPD)**
  McLean County, Illinois (EXSL 1994)

The program was designed for the purpose of providing the county court system with an alternative to secure detention. The EPD targeted a specific population of minors, aged 11 to 17, who were involved with the juvenile justice system. The program allows minors who should be in secure custody an opportunity to remain in the community by providing the structure that a detention center provides, but in a nonsecure setting.

■ **Facilities Action Strategy Team (F.A.S.T.)**
City of New York, New York (EXSL 1989)

A team of architects, engineers, and tradesmen serve as the in-house construction group of New York City's Bureau of Facilities Management, providing a time-efficient and cost-effective alternative to the city's capital process for emergency construction and facilities redesign. The utilization of F.A.S.T. has saved the city money, increased the quality of construction, and ultimately improved city services in a wide variety of projects.

■ **Farming Safely in the Thumb**
Huron County, Michigan (EXSL 1992)

Farming Safely in the Thumb provides safety education and training to farmers and their family members. This prevention program is responding to the new challenges faced by farm workers, such as pesticides and new technologies. Its goal is the reduction of agriculture-related injuries/deaths. The program helps identify hazards and provides recommendations toward eliminating them or increasing skills for dealing with those that cannot be eliminated.

■ **Fast Track Residential Street Reconstruction Program**
Village of Schaumburg, Illinois (EXSL 1989)

A computerized pavement management system "fast tracks" and evaluates the status of street repair. By coordinating public works projects, it significantly improves response time, minimizes deferred maintenance costs, and reduces property damage. Substantial residential, commercial, and industrial growth resulted.

■ **Friends for Life**
Albuquerque, New Mexico (EXSL 1992)

The Friends for Life program establishes a new base level of services for committed juveniles through the use of volunteers and community services and resources. This new array of intermediate services provided by the volunteers includes basic nurturing, friendship, companionship, role modeling, mentoring, and nonformal surrogate family relationships.

From this new base level, the more traditional program and therapeutic services can be launched and administered more effectively.

■ **General Relief Interagency Project (GRIP)**
  Ventura County, California (EXSL 1994)

The GRIP is an integrated service delivery system for general relief (GR) clients in Ventura County, California. The intent of the program is to reduce the length of time an individual stays on GR and to gain reimbursement of costs by assisting clients with the social security process. The GRIP program coordinates a variety of services needed by GR recipients to assist them to leave the program as quickly as possible.

■ **Governor's Guaranteed Work Force Program**
  State of West Virginia (EXSL 1991)

To improve the ability of state businesses to compete in the national and global marketplace, the program assists new and existing companies of all sizes to expand or upgrade competitive or technical skills of current employees through versatile, one-stop centers for all available government training programs. Customized services meet employee and company needs.

■ **Greensboro's Affordable Housing Vision**
  Greensboro, North Carolina (EXSL 1992)

Greensboro's Affordable Housing Vision is funded by the Greensboro Housing Partnership Trust Fund, which was created by the allocation of one cent of the city's ad valorem tax for the exclusive use of affordable housing initiatives. This unique funding program grew out of the community's awareness of the need for affordable housing in Greensboro and its commitment to fund this prioritized need.

■ **Hanover Health Plan**
  Town of Hanover, Massachusetts (EXSL 1991)

Faced with a 49% increase in premiums for health insurance for employees, which translated into a 9.5% loss in pay, the town designed a unique plan with high deductible and copayment insurance, combined with a self-insuring trust fund and a modest reimbursement procedure.

All employees have quality coverage with substantial savings to the town, enabling administration to maintain a full level of personnel.

■ **Heart of Milwaukee Initiative**
  Madison, Wisconsin (EXSL 1994)

The Wisconsin Housing and Economic Development Authority created the Heart of Milwaukee Initiative to increase home ownership in the central city. Milwaukee was identified as having the highest ratio in the nation of mortgage rejections for blacks as compared to whites. The program was designed to gain the support of city officials as well as community leaders to promote home ownership in an effort to stabilize the core of the city. In addition, the support of local lending institutions was secured in order to provide affordable financing for minorities interested in purchasing homes in the central city.

■ **Hillsborough County Health Care Plan**
  Hillsborough County, Florida (EXSL 1995)

The Hillsborough Health Care Plan has increased access to quality health care; improved the integration of medical, mental health, and social services; enhanced prevention and education; and reduced per-patient expenditures. The number of primary care sites has increased from 4 to 16, and the number of patients served annually has risen from 15,000 to 24,000. The service has diverted 11,456 potential emergency room visits at an estimated cost avoidance of over $5,700,000 in 2 years.

■ **Housing Vermont**
  Vermont Housing Agency (EXSL 1990)

Housing Vermont is a statewide, nonprofit corporation created by the Vermont Housing Agency in 1988 to preserve and/or develop affordable rental housing for its citizens and also to foster innovative relationships between public and private interests for affordable housing. An important and innovative component is the Vermont Equity Fund, an investment vehicle designed to give corporate investors an opportunity for relatively low-risk investments in housing.

■ **Hudson County AIDS Network of Care**
Hudson County, New Jersey (EXSL 1992)

Hudson County, New Jersey, has the second highest per capita incidence of HIV/AIDS in the United States. The Hudson County AIDS
Network of Care responds to the epidemic by means of a comprehensive
system of care, providing for early detection and treatment for HIV/AIDS.
A systems approach is utilized that requires the county, and municipalities
within the county, to share fiscal and community resources.

■ **Improving Ambulance Operations: A Blueprint for Change**
District of Columbia (EXSL 1990)

The District of Columbia undertook a major operations improvements project involving the District's emergency medical services (EMS)
system with help from the District's internal management consulting
arm, Productivity Management Services. It represents an agenda for
change in strategic and operational areas, and provides a framework for
making key operational and strategic decisions that will ultimately result
in a higher quality, more reliable, and more efficient EMS.

■ **Information Network of Kansas (INK)**
Topeka, Kansas (EXSL 1992)

INK provides on-line computer access to public information to the
citizens of Kansas. INK has more than 2,000 subscribers, accessing 83
on-line applications consisting of over 100 separate information sources
within Kansas's state, county, and local governments. Today's system can
be accessed via modem with an IBM-PC or a Macintosh. A regulated fee
of $.40 per minute is charged the subscriber for electronic access to the
public information.

■ **Innovation in Recruiting and Hiring:**
Attracting the "Best and Brightest" to State Service
State of Wisconsin (EXSL 1994)

The hiring innovations pioneered by the Wisconsin Department of
Employment Relations provide Wisconsin's state agencies and citizens
with more efficient, responsive, and "user-friendly" civil service hiring
systems. These innovations—the Entry Professional Program, the Criti-

cal Recruitment Program, Walk-in Civil Service Testing, and JOBS (Job Opportunity Bulletin System)—have greatly enhanced the state government's success in hiring highly qualified employees who reflect the state's diversity.

■ **Innovative Military Projects and Career Training (IMPACT)**
State of California (EXSL 1991)

To address the pressing needs of 17- to 21-year-old undereducated, at-risk urban youth, a highly structured 6-week education and job preparation model encompasses basic, premilitary, and preemployment skills provided by a combination of National Guard and civilian instructors was developed. The IMPACT program, designed as an alternative to incarceration, saves the state money and provides participants with employment, military, and training opportunities.

■ **Integrating Bar Code Technology With Curbside Recycling**
City of St. Louis Park, Minnesota (EXSL 1991)

To solve a landfill problem by encouraging recycling, residents are rewarded with lower garbage bills, with amounts determined by hand-held computers used to scan bar code stickers on residents' recycling bins. Voluntary recycling participation has increased from 45% to 90% in response to the financial incentive; 38% of garbage (including yard waste) is diverted from the landfill; refuse hauling costs are lower; the investment for bar coding paid for itself in 10 months.

■ **Intensive Supervision Program**
State of New Jersey (EXSL 1991)

To prevent prison overcrowding and to screen nonviolent offenders for early release, a highly structured community release program was established. It encompasses electronic and substance abuse monitoring, full-time employment, community service, and repayment of court-ordered payments of fines and penalties.

■ **Interagency Coordination**
Houston, Texas (EXSL 1994)

Interagency Coordination made it possible to coordinate the major capital improvement projects undertaken by various city, county, and state agencies in the Greater Houston area. The opportunity to make interagency cooperation viable began soon after the start of the Greater Houston Wastewater Program (GHWP), a Division of the city's Department of Public Works and Engineering.

■ **Intergovernmental Computer Link-Up**
City of Phoenix, Arizona (EXSL 1990)

Due to the long delays often experienced by individuals applying to the City of Phoenix Neighborhood Improvement and Housing Department (NIH), the agency established the program Intergovernmental Computer Link-Up to better facilitate the application process and reduce duplication of effort, delays, and clerical costs to the city. Due to unacceptable waiting times, delays, fraud, and other procedural problems, the agency endeavored to link up formerly incompatible computer systems between the Department of Economic Security and the NIH.

■ **Iowa Corps**
Iowa Department of Economic Development (EXSL 1990)

This program encourages high school students to perform community service work for nonprofit organizations; provides incentives for Iowa youth to attend Iowa colleges and universities; and helps prevent the further out-migration of Iowa youth. High school students throughout the state are encouraged to apply for this incentive-based scholarship, which in return for community service, rewards each successful applicant with $500 toward post-secondary education within the state.

■ **King County Correctional Facility Mental Health Committee**
King County, Washington (EXSL 1990)

Due to the increasing number of incarcerated persons who suffer from mental illness, the King County Department of Adult Detention established the King County Correctional Facility Mental Health Committee program to address the different needs of mentally ill offenders in public prisons. The mental health committee is charged with enhancing the availability of mental health services to prisoners while incarcerated and upon their release. The program has improved the quality of life of mentally ill offenders by establishing support mechanisms, de-emphasizing the punitive nature of incarceration, and promising the offender continuation of care upon release.

■ **L.A. County Telecommuting-Telework Program**
Los Angeles County, California (EXSL 1995)

The primary objective of this program is to promote a more productive work-at-home or near-home work option for employees who commute long distances to their work places. Labor representatives were consulted and a telecommuting agreement was negotiated outlining employer/ employee responsibilities. The agreement is supported by behavior change and workplace alternatives training models.

■ **Land Reutilization Commission**
Douglas County, Nebraska (EXSL 1991)

To return tax delinquent land to tax roles in order to provide affordable housing, new industry, jobs, and new revenue, the commission sells vacant property based on appraised value with current title owners having the option of retaining property if all taxes owed are paid before transfer occurs. In 3 years, the commission has returned approximately $2.1 million to taxing authorities. The low overhead for operations has resulted in the return of additional monies to local authorities.

■ **Law Enforcement Evaluations**
City of Paramount, California (EXSL 1989)

A citizen survey and evaluation system resulted in improved law enforcement services, increased accountability, enhanced service delivery, more productive community interaction, and reduced crime levels. Evaluation forms are given to every victim or complaining party to assess courtesy and competency. The evaluations proved that despite the number of complaints, residents overwhelming appreciated the protection they received. Feeling appreciated rather than maligned has resulted in improved performance and morale for law enforcement personnel.

■ **Law Enforcement Property Recovery Unit**
State of Florida (EXSL 1990)

In response to the growing incidence of property crimes in Florida, local law enforcement officials have begun to coordinate their efforts in an attempt to track and recover stolen property, and to prosecute the individuals responsible for the crimes. The program coordinates a number of facets of theft investigation, including scrutinizing the records of transactions of local pawnshops, jewelry stores, and other legitimate business across jurisdictional borders.

■ **Life Enhancement Alternative Program**
Salt Lake County, Utah (EXSL 1995)

The Life Enhancement Alternative Program (L.E.A.P) is a court-sanctioned project designed to provide early intervention to youths 14 years of age and younger with minor delinquent offenses. L.E.A.P is offered free of charge and is part of the Salt Lake County Division of Youth Services. This 60-day program includes weekly law-related education classes, individual and family therapy, school tracking, and a community service project.

■ **Local Government Program**
State of Texas (EXSL 1989)

The Texas Comptroller's Office provides a manual to help city and county governments set up a standard accounting system. A team of consultants provides city, county, and other local officials with technical assistance in the interpretation of the maze of changing state laws and regulations. Assistance also includes telephone consultations, seminars, manuals, and a plain-English newsletter.

■ **Maintenance Reserve Program**
Kansas City, Missouri (EXSL 1994)

The Maintenance Reserve Program (MIRP) was developed to complement Kansas City's Rehabilitation Loan Program (RLP), operated by the nonprofit Rehabilitation Loan Corporation. Essentially, the MIRP is health insurance for the home. This program offers nontraditional homeowner insurance to low-income residents, for a nominal fee, that enables them to maintain their homes.

■ Management by Unreasonable Objectives
City of Dayton, Ohio (EXSL 1995)

A new technique, Management by Unreasonable Objectives (MBUO), is a system that is used selectively to create significant change. MBUO promotes innovation and encourages employees to think "outside the box." Hard results of these initiatives are substantial productivity, growth, increased revenues, and an efficient and proud staff.

■ Mayor's Handicap Parking Enforcement Team
City of Flint, Michigan (EXSL 1989)

In light of insufficient police personnel levels, this program trains and authorizes volunteers to educate the public as to the use of handicap parking spaces and to issue tickets to violators. As a result of budget constraints due to a high unemployment rate and decline in population, the Flint Police Department experienced a dramatic reduction in force. Combined with a high rate of crime, the enforcement of handicap parking laws became a low priority. The Volunteer Enforcement Team is totally self-supporting and actually generates revenue for the city.

■ Medicaid Waiver Project
State of Tennessee (EXSL 1990)

This program addresses the need to provide additional long-term community care to mentally retarded adults 18 years of age and older, at costs less than those associated with institutionalization. The Waiver project proved cost-effective throughout the first 2 years of operation by saving $8 million dollars in Medicaid costs. The project also established a complaint handling system to report any problems with community-based providers, with no substantial complaints registered.

■ Medical Care for Children Project
Fairfax County, Virginia (EXSL 1989)

This public-private partnership provides very low cost medical services to children from indigent families who lack Medicaid, health insurance, cash, or other resources to pay for health care. The goals of the program are to reduce the incidence of and consequences of late, inadequate, or lack of treatment of children's illnesses and to facilitate family efforts to become self-supporting.

■ **Medical Quality Assurance Program**
  Lee County, Fort Meyers, Florida (EXSL 1989)

A comprehensive medical quality assurance program is designed to achieve and maintain an optimal level of pre-hospital patient care. Prior to the implementation of this program, problems of improper patient care were dealt with in a reactionary nature. This program significantly decreases the likelihood of costly medical malpractice litigation.

■ **Metropass Program**
  State of Florida (EXSL 1994)

The Medicaid Metropass Program, a joint venture by the State of Florida Agency for Health Care Administration and the Metro Dade County Transit Agency, was designed to provide unlimited public transportation to selected Medicaid recipients who forgo the use of their individualized Medicaid transportation to medical appointments.

■ **A Model for Capping Wage and Benefit Costs**
  Marion County, Oregon (EXSL 1992)

Marion County and its largest union have developed a model for negotiating wages and benefits that places a cap on the employer's future expenditures. The model defines the employer's maximum future personnel service costs while giving the union flexibility to bargain changes in salaries, insurance, and other employee benefits.

■ **Move to Independence Program**
  Los Angeles County, California (EXSL 1991)

As part of the rehabilitation plan for hard-core, incarcerated male juvenile offenders (ages 16-18), a unique partnership has been formed by the county probation department and the county Office of Education. Since inception of the program in 1990, handicapped students have achieved 141% average improvement in seven functional motor skills.

"Camp Wards," the juvenile offenders, have developed compassion, self-worth, and marketable skills in the health care and education fields.

■ Neighborhood Pride and Protection Program
San Diego, California (EXSL 1994)

The Public Library plays an integral role in the City of San Diego's Neighborhood Pride and Protection Program (NPP). Developed in 1991, the program is dedicated to enhancing the quality of life for all San Diegans by forming community partnerships within neighborhoods to broaden the scope and impact of city services. The San Diego Public Library's NPP program addresses the underlying programs associated with at-risk youth, ages 4 through 18.

■ New Jersey Hazardous Material Training Program
New Jersey State Police (EXSL 1992)

This program develops, maintains, and administers training courses in hazardous materials response that comply with, or exceed, standards established under state mandate. The training is provided to public sector employees who respond to accidents and other emergency situations where there is the potential for the release of hazardous substances.

■ A New Lease on Life
Colorado Department of Institutions (EXSL 1990)

In keeping with the movement toward providing alternatives to institutionalizing the mentally disabled, the Colorado Department of Institutions established a program of public housing designed to meet specifically the needs of persons with mental disabilities through rehabilitating existing housing stock.

■ New York State Partnership for Long-Term Care
State of New York (EXSL 1995)

The New York State (NYS) Partnership for Long Term Care, implemented in 1993, emphasizes shared responsibility for financing long-term care (LTC) by offering New Yorkers an alternative way to pay for their LTC. The premise of the Partnership is that it holds the potential of significant savings to the Medicaid program over time as more people, who would have spent down or transferred their assets absent the program, purchase LTC insurance.

■ **North East Alzheimer's Day Care/Home Care Center**
  City of Deerfield Beach, Florida (EXSL 1991)

An increasing population of cognitively impaired persons, and recognition of the extent of unmet needs, was the basis for creating a specialized facility with a broad range of supports through joint efforts of the city, Broward County, and a volunteer task force to help patients and caregivers in a cost-effective service. Expensive, long-term care institutionalization is being delayed for some 150 Alzheimer victims a year, and 150 caregivers are receiving 50,000+ hours of respite and counseling at minimal cost to taxpayers.

■ **Note Sale Directly to Residents**
  Township of Parsipanny-Troy Hills, New Jersey (EXSL 1989)

This program provided the opportunity for residents to purchase one-year tax exempt bonds directly through the township. These general obligation notes were specifically issued to finance the final phase of a flood control project within the township. The emphasis of this program was to allow "very small" township investors the opportunity to participate in the fund-raising activities of their community.

■ **Operation Border Crossing**
  Port Authority of New York & New Jersey (EXSL 1992)

The Port Authority Police, in cooperation with Bergen County (New Jersey) police officers, conduct surveillance of suspected drug buyers as they make purchases in the Washington Heights section of New York. The unique aspect of this program is that it involves a cooperative effort between members of New York and New Jersey police departments in an effort to reduce the drug traffic over the George Washington Bridge.

■ **Operation Fatherhood**
  State of New Jersey (EXSL 1995)

First Steps, Union Industrial Home's first teen fathers program, is designed to provide inner-city males between the ages of 13 and 19 with the skills and motivation to become successfully independent, healthy, and socially responsible young men. The project is one of nine pilot sites, nationwide, selected to test the effectiveness of job training and supportive services for noncustodial fathers (between the ages of 16 and 45) whose children receive welfare.

■ **Operation Hand Up**
  State of Hawaii (EXSL 1992)

Operation Hand Up offers a helping hand to employable individuals by giving them clean, subsistent housing, laundry and shower facilities, and one hot meal a day for $200 a month. In addition, job training and counseling for drug or alcohol abuse, stress management, and other personal problems is provided.

■ **Operations Improvement and Development Program**
  Hillsborough County, Florida (EXSL 1989)

This program implements quality-productivity strategies of enhanced public service delivery through strategic planning and goal setting; application of new productivity techniques and skills; enhanced employee and management competency; automation; performance measurement; and planned value and cultural changes in the organization.

■ **Orange County Community Distribution Project**
  Orange County, Florida (EXSL 1995)

The Orange County Community Distribution Center (OCCDC) opened in 1993 as a private-public partnership to: (a) reduce waste of construction materials that would otherwise go to the landfill; (b) provide a central clearinghouse for donations of surplus usable construction materials from individuals and the construction industry; (c) provide a continuing source of free building materials to eligible nonprofit agencies; and (d) provide training in warehouse operations for minimum risk offenders, using meaningful work experiences.

■ **Orange County Fleet Management Productivity Improvement Plan**
  Orange County, Florida (EXSL 1994)

Faced with a 66% growth in fleet size and a growth in staff size of less than 5%, the Orange County Department of Fleet Management needed a nonmonetary means of increasing production. Labor and management decided to implement a variety of programs to increase productivity, improve customer satisfaction, and save taxpayer dollars. Programs such as employee participation in the hiring process, total quality management, expansion of working hours, job rotation, in-house GED training, conflict resolution, and a feedback production control program produced measurable results.

■ **Park Place Senior Center**
  Village of Arlington Heights, Illinois (EXSL 1989)

A formal community partnership helps promote independence and quality of life for senior citizens. Eight different agencies work together out of one central location—a multipurpose senior center—to provide a wide array of services to the elderly in a cost effective manner. Colocation and the development of community partnerships has proven that working together is extremely cost-effective, and agencies can better enhance their programs by pooling resources.

■ **Partners in Productivity**
  State of Florida (EXSL 1991)

This program institutionalizes productivity improvement through a public-private cooperative initiative to identify, implement, measure, and reward major cost savings and performance enhancements in state government. Cost saving and management improvement recommendations have saved over $100 million. Employees have become engaged in total quality management methods.

■ **Payment-in-Lieu of Tax Program (PILOT)**
  City of Boston, Massachusetts (EXSL 1991)

Over half of the land area in the City of Boston is tax exempt. The PILOT program was designed to provide Boston with some benefits in an equitable manner for the municipal services provided to the numerous tax-exempt institutions. The PILOT program introduced changes in the tax base that resulted in over $10 million in revenue in 1990. The number of exempt properties decreased and the community services portion of the program provided over $6 million in benefits to residents—at the partial cost of the salary of one employee.

■ **Perinatal Outreach Program**
Alameda County, California (EXSL 1990)

Alameda County Social Services Agency piloted a program to outstation Medi-Cal eligibility workers at county and community prenatal clinics. The resulting program improved access to prenatal care and has become a state model for informing uninsured women of the importance of prenatal care and intervention, and then enrolling these women for Medi-Cal benefits. This program has succeeded in coordinating the efforts of the county health care and social services agencies toward the common goal of increasing access to prenatal care for at-risk women.

■ **Personnel Pilot Project**
State of Florida (EXSL 1992)

The Division of Workers' Compensation achieved increases in productivity, quality, and customer satisfaction by streamlining the classification and pay plan, flattening the organizational structure, developing monetary and nonmonetary employee incentive programs, and creating innovative training and career development projects.

■ **Please Be Seated**
State of Virginia (EXSL 1991)

To prevent death or injury to young children in motor vehicle accidents, a statewide educational program was instituted. A cooperative effort involving parents, rescue squads, medical personnel, cooperative extension, teachers, business owners, and others, the program teaches the importance of properly securing children, combined with a free safety seat program. Fatalities have decreased markedly.

■ Prison Braille Project
Bucks County, Pennsylvania (EXSL 1995)

Blind students in Bucks County found it very difficult to excel in
regular classes because of a lack of adequate braille materials. Teachers
had to spend inordinate amounts of time to braille text books and other
materials needed by blind students. The funds from the Lion/Lioness
Clubs allowed the acquisition of special software and computer hardware. Instead of teachers having to do so, inmates now braille textbooks,
workbooks, and dittos. This cooperative effort not only increased the
involvement and productivity of blind students, but also the productivity
of inmates involved in the project. Teachers now have more time to
dedicate to classroom teaching and inmates are learning a valuable skill.

■ Process Improvement Initiative
State of Arizona (EXSL 1994)

The Process Improvement Initiative is a systematic effort to improve
the child support collection system in the state of Arizona. The Process
Improvement Initiative (PII) did not focus on restructuring the organization, but rather on replacing outdated, ineffective processes with those
that would increase the number of child support orders established and
enforced, decrease cycle time, and provide exemplary customer service.

■ A Program for Successful Risk Management
Town of Culpepper, Virginia (EXSL 1992)

In a unique methodology format that risk managers can utilize to
obtain a realistic picture of the results of their programs, the Town of
Culpepper reduced insurance costs by 39.1%. Before the initiation of
this program, the town's worker compensation costs were escalating out
of control. The town was in an assigned risk pool and injuries were
mounting.

■ Program Measurement System
City of St. Petersburg, Florida (EXSL 1989)

A centrally coordinated systematic approach for objectively obtaining
and evaluating information regarding the performance of city programs
against established objectives, this program provides outcome measures

to policymakers for purposes of management, budgeting, and accountability. It requires city management to focus on results rather than
activities, and provides information needed by city council, city management team, and departmental personnel to make informed decisions, as
well as informing the public of program accomplishments.

■ **Programmed Tree Pruning**
City of Modesto, California (EXSL 1991)

The City of Modesto developed a tree maintenance program that over
a 10-year period has increased production threefold and significantly
reduced the city's liability exposure due to tree failures. A systematic
pruning cycle has brought the health of the urban forest to its highest
level in years; citizen compliments have replaced complaints; crews work
in self-directed work teams; productivity has increased 15%; the urban
forest has increased to 95,000 trees.

■ **Quality Improvement Program**
Pinellas County, Florida (EXSL 1990)

Pinellas County established a comprehensive quality improvement
program to facilitate greater employee involvement and improved municipal services to county residents. The objective of the county government is to effect increased employee productivity with an eye toward
quality and efficiency. Employee participation is the cornerstone of this
effort, which rewards achievements with monetary incentives as well as
gifts, paid leave, and public recognition. Within 2 years, the county
realized over $650,000 in savings through the more efficient use of
resources, time management, and employee-generated innovations.

■ **Residential Police Officer Program**
Alexandria, Virginia (EXSL 1994)

The Alexandria Police Department introduced the Residential Police
Officer (RPO) Program in the fall of 1992 as a pilot program aimed at
reducing serious crime in one of the city's most vulnerable neighborhoods. In the RPO program, a veteran police officer moves into a selected
public housing community or other low-income neighborhood, which
becomes the Residential Police Officer's patrol "beat."

■ **Rightsizing Financial Plan**
City of Corvallis, Oregon (EXSL 1991)

The city undertook a 5-year fiscal plan in 1991 to ensure cost-effectiveness and maintain services through rigorous self-examination and realignment using rightsizing strategic planning techniques. Citizens are customers and stockholders in the Corvallis Municipal Corporation; supervisor-to-employee ratios were reduced; the budget was reduced 34% without service eliminations; city bonds were rated A; water and property tax rates were reduced.

■ **River of Dreams**
City of Phoenix, Arizona (EXSL 1992)

River of Dreams is the first National Park Service sanctioned Grand Canyon raft program for people with significant physical, medical, and mental disabilities. The City of Phoenix collaborated with nonprofit organizations and commercial outfitters to pioneer this landmark program of accessibility. Trips are offered to people with disabilities, illustrating that the nation's natural environment is everyone's birthright.

■ **Salt Lake County Business/Government Alliance**
Salt Lake County, Utah (EXSL 1989)

A public-private partnership composed of members of the business community and government, plans, studies, and implements solutions to common problems facing the county and local business, with the goal of maintaining, preserving, and improving the quality of life.

■ **Sanitary Sewer Infiltration/Inflow Prevention**
Johnson County, Mission, Kansas (EXSL 1989)

Using a design innovation, a collection system was redesigned to reduce sanitary sewer backups in homes and buildings, and to prevent bypasses to streams during moderate and heavy rainfalls. Comparing the replacement of sewers with the redesign and rehabilitation of the existing system and watersheds, the county realized a cost-savings of over $65 million dollars.

■ **School Based Youth Services Program**
   State of New Jersey (EXSL 1994)

Implemented in 1988 under Governor Thomas Kean, the New Jersey School Based Youth Services Program (SBYSP) provides comprehensive services on a one-stop-shopping basis in or near secondary schools. The SBYSP helped to eliminate artificial boundaries between schools and various human service, health, and employment systems by creating a link among service providers that fosters a comprehensive system of care for at-risk youth. Sites provide the following core services: health care; mental health and family counseling; employment training; and substance abuse counseling.

■ **Schools in the Age of Technology**
   Hunterdon County, New Jersey (EXSL 1995)

Hunterdon Central School District has made a commitment to educating students to be self-directed learners by equipping the facility to provide school-on-demand. These goals have been achieved through a campuswide fiber optic backbone; classroom computers, telephones, and video receivers; student-run TV and radio stations broadcasting to the classrooms and the community; and four state-of-the-art prototype classrooms: physics, applied technology, biochemistry, and fine arts.

■ **SCROOGE Program (Support Children,**
   Remember Obligations, or Get Embarrassed)
   Chautauqua County, New York (EXSL 1990)

This project reduces the number of delinquent child support payments, relying upon negative public exposure to compel legally responsible relatives to meet their financial obligations. Due to an increasing problem of noncompliance relative to court-ordered child support payments, the program was designed to use the threat of negative media exposure during the holiday season, hence the name Scrooge, to make both the public and the offender aware that noncompliance would not be tolerated.

■ **Self-Help Support System**
State of New York (EXSL 1992)

The New York State Self-Help Support System is a joint partnership
of the Department of State, the Department of Environmental Conservation and Health, the Environmental Facilities Corporation, and The
Rensselaerville Institute. This innovative and dynamic technical assistance team, the only public-private coalition of its kind the country,
provides expertise to alleviate water and wastewater problems of small
communities.

■ **Service Enhancement Program**
City of San Diego, California (EXSL 1989)

In the face of serious budget cutbacks resulting from Proposition 13,
San Diego enhanced services while maintaining the commitment to
service by city employees. The challenge of maintaining productivity
after serious budget cuts was met through the development of performance measures, citywide training in customer service philosophy and
techniques, and the inclusion of customer service function and standards
in each employee's performance evaluation.

■ **Shared Aide Services: Cost Effective Home Care**
Erie County, New York (EXSL 1992)

Erie County was able to conserve Medicaid funds, enhance client
independence, and use personal care aides more effectively through the
utilization of a more efficient model for home care service delivery. The
program confronts the difficult challenge of administering a quality
home care program in the face of escalating costs and a shortage of
personal care aides.

■ **Shared Savings Project**
City of Pittsburg, California (EXSL 1989)

This project utilizes the principles of worker participation, financial
incentives, quality measurement, and employee awareness of the real cost
of service delivery to increase performance and reduce cost for maintenance services. Private sector incentives linked to employee compensa-

tion resulted in increased efficiency and utilization of equipment, supplies, and labor resources.

■ **S.M.A.R.T. (Separate Materials and Recycle Together)**
City of Wilmington, North Carolina (EXSL 1990)

Focusing on community involvement and interlocal agreements, this program collects, processes, and sells recyclable materials. It avoids substantial disposal costs at local landfills and waste-to-energy incinerators.

■ **South Florida Water Management District**
Productivity Improvement Program
State of Florida (EXSL 1992)

The South Florida Water Management District (SFWMD) Productivity Improvement Program (PIP) is a comprehensive design that addresses a critical need in response to widespread public demands for optimal utilization of scarce governmental resources. A substantive productivity improvement program enhances the supply of South Florida water.

■ **Sparkling Water System, Largo Reclaimed Water Project**
City of Largo, Florida (EXSL 1995)

The City of Largo's solution to water supply problems involves using an alternate source of water for nonessential purposes, such as irrigation. The program conserves drinking water (e.g., reclaimed water is used in air conditioning cooling towers), decreases effluent discharge into Tampa Bay, and replenishes water being withdrawn from the Floridan Aquifer.

■ **STARR Program**
State of North Carolina (EXSL 1992)

The STARR (Substance Treatment and Recidivism Reduction) Program is a substance abuse treatment, life skills education, and community referral program designed to keep a targeted inmate population in recovery and out of jail. During the 4-week program, 20 local agencies work directly with inmates, addressing issues of financial, social, medical, legal, housing, family, educational, and recovery needs.

■ **State Health Insurance Program (SHIP)**
  State of Hawaii (EXSL 1991)

Through a partnership of the state and the private sector, and utilizing sliding-scale premiums, SHIP subsidizes residents who did not qualify for any form of health insurance. Under SHIP, tens of thousands of Hawaiians are covered; a major provider has decreased premium rates; increased benefits have been added; and no-cost linkages with other services have been established.

■ **Statewide Long-term Improved Management (Project SLIM)**
  State of Arizona (EXSL 1992)

Project SLIM was designed to streamline state government and improve the quality of services delivered by implementing successful management principles. Working through state employees, a report detailing over 300 recommendations within the 12 largest state agencies was compiled. A private sector steering committee oversaw teams of state employees, who were trained by outside consultants to implement the recommendations.

■ **Stormwater Management Retrofit Program**
  City of Baltimore, Maryland (EXSL 1990)

This citywide retrofit program sought to modify seven stormwater structures for phosphorus and algae removal, eradicating the problem of low dissolved oxygen. Growing urbanization contributed to the problem of water quality, and the main thrust of this program was to improve the overall quality of the city's water supply.

■ **Strategic Planning for Unified Decision Support**
  City of Fremont, California (EXSL 1989)

SPUDS is a ground-up strategic planning process. All city government departments construct a strategic plan, allowing them to evaluate their environments and plan for improved responses to citizen needs. An integrated interdepartmental strategic plan responds to the need for a long-term vision and the development of cooperation across departments in order to implement the plan.

■ **Substance Abuse Information System**
  Baltimore County, Maryland (EXSL 1994)

Baltimore County's Substance Abuse Information System is a computerized on-line data collection and billing system that follows each client admitted into the substance abuse program throughout his or her treatment plan. It is user-friendly and maintains a master registration record that allows multiple admissions to be entered for each client. The system is capable of generating reports on virtually any combination of criteria. Since its implementation in 1989, the Baltimore County Office of Substance Abuse has been able to increase its effectiveness in treating substance-abuse clients and has increased annual revenues from $330,000 to over $550,000 in 4 years.

■ **Tax Assistance Workshops**
  State of Texas (EXSL 1995)

By helping low-income working families to complete income tax forms and apply for the earned income credit (EIC), volunteers are increasing the economic well-being of their clients. The goal is to assist people who cannot afford to pay someone to complete their tax returns, and to inform and educate about EIC and how to apply. Earned income credit was designed to increase family financial stability and help working people maintain independence from the "welfare" system, and that is the ultimate goal of this program.

■ **T.E.A.C.H. Early Childhood Project**
  Chapel Hill, North Carolina (EXSL 1994)

The T.E.A.C.H. project is based on the principle of partnership and brings together the statewide community college system, child care staff, employing agencies, and scholarship program as well as partnering many diverse funding sources. The project's goal is to make a positive change in the quality of care that children who are cared for in child care centers throughout North Carolina receive by addressing some of the issues that have resulted in a statewide, and indeed national, child care staffing crisis.

■ **Telefile: Filing Taxes by Phone**
  State of Massachusetts (EXSL 1995)

Telefile allows taxpayers to file their state income taxes via Touch-Tone telephone, and was born from the recognition that services were ready for innovative changes. The cost of processing a Telefile return will ultimately reduce DOR costs by 80%. Taxpayers can access the program 24 hours a day and can expect their refunds within 4 days. An innovative component of Telefile is the Prize Program. Funded by private donations, it was designed to encourage taxpayers to participate in Telefile and to reward them for filing early.

■ **Tenant Assistance Program (TAP)**
  State of Massachusetts (EXSL 1991)

To improve tenants' quality of life and to preserve affordable housing through addressing drug and alcohol abuse, the Massachusetts Housing Finance Agency created TAP to train all property management staff in prevention and intervention techniques, coupled with tenant education and crisis intervention services. It has saved nearly $1 million in insurance premium discounts, resulted in the formation of resident associations, and developed effective crisis intervention.

■ **Tidewater Regional Technical Rescue Team**
  City of Virginia Beach, Virginia (EXSL 1991)

In response to a growing need for highly technical types of rescues, a low-cost regional team was organized utilizing municipal, military, and nonprofit organization resources to respond to the Tidewater area and national catastrophic emergencies. A highly trained force is available 365 days a year to provide technical rescue services to five cities and all military installations in a 2,000 square mile area. A nonprofit organization raises and manages funds for equipment; personnel costs are absorbed locally.

■ **Training Information and Resource Center (TIRC)**
  State of Illinois (EXSL 1991)

To provide cost-effective training to the 3,000 employees of the Illinois Department of Employment Security, line-driven training has been instituted with a two-level approach through the creation of TIRC in conjunction with Anderson Consultants as a partner. Individuals' personal growth has been facilitated and agency-specific training for groups of employees has been implemented for 50% of the department's workforce; employees participate in curriculum development; TIRC trains pools of employees to serve as trainers.

■ **Trenton Office of Policy Studies (TOPS)**
  Trenton, New Jersey (EXSL 1994)

The Trenton Office of Policy Studies (TOPS) was created by the City of Trenton and Thomas Edison State College as an innovative partnership to analyze emerging issues of public policy that affect the residents of Trenton. TOPS was designed to be proactive in assisting the city government in formulating programs and plans to address these issues.

■ **United Methodist Army Repair Project**
  State of Texas (EXSL 1995)

United Methodist Army (U.M. Army) Reach-Out Mission by Youth is part of the Texas Conference of the United Methodist Church. Its mission is to minister to needy Texans who are registered with the Texas Department of Human Services Community Care for the Aged and Disabled Services Program. It meets the structural and home repair needs of persons with disabilities, the elderly, and the homeless, and marshals additional resources for this purpose. The program is entirely self-supporting, since volunteers donate labor and pay their own expenses.

■ **Value Engineering for Clean Water Program**
  San Diego, California (EXSL 1992)

Value engineering (VE) study is a tool for evaluating the cost-effectiveness, reliability, quality, and safety of a design project. The Clean Water Program has undergone nine VE studies, resulting in savings of more than $70 million. Problems found were evaluated, new design proposals were suggested, and changes and modifications were made to ensure performance, reliability, quality, and safety.

■ **Vendor Information Program (VIP)**
State of Oregon (EXSL 1992)

VIP is the first automated bid access program in the country. Vendors, using an IBM-compatible personal computer and modem, can access current and historical bid information 24 hours a day, 7 days a week. Vendors can view and download purchasing information in the convenience of their own office. VIP replaced 50 years of a public purchasing protocol that was encumbered with a labor-intensive, cost-prohibitive, paper-bid distribution system.

■ **Victim Offender Mediation Program**
Albuquerque, New Mexico (EXSL 1992)

This model program reinforces cognitive and problem-solving skills for juvenile offenders. It helps youth to understand the human impact of their actions from an emotional as well as material aspect. It enables offenders to experience responsibility and accountability for their behavior. The program is a partnership between a nonprofit agency and the local juvenile probation and parole office, a public agency. Statistics show offenders are more likely to complete their restitution obligation through this program than through a court-ordered restitution.

■ **Volunteer Interpreter Service**
State of Texas (EXSL 1994)

Lack of interpreters often creates a loss of communication between Texas Department of Human Services (TDHS) staff and non-English-speaking applicants for Food Stamps, Medicaid, and Aid to Families with Dependent Children. This causes errors in work and disrupts service. This is the guiding force behind the creation of the Volunteer Interpreter Service.

■ **Volunteer Service Program**
Visalia, California (EXSL 1990)

The Volunteer Service Program of Visalia, California, was created in 1986 when the city merged its internal government volunteer program with two local volunteer organizations to create the only comprehensive government-funded volunteer program in California. It extends a volunteer network to any nonprofit, government, or community service organization.

■ **Washington Interactive Television**
State of Washington (EXSL 1994)

Washington Interactive Television (WIT) is Washington state's public video telecommunications system. WIT serves elected officials, state agencies, municipal governments, public schools, higher education, and citizens to make communication faster, easier, less expensive, and more effective. The value of WIT for saving time and money, increasing access to government, and bettering statewide communication has been proven in numerous ways.

■ **Washington State Department of Personnel**
State of Washington (EXSL 1995)

The Washington State Department of Personnel recently implemented two innovative initiatives designed to attract the "best and brightest" to public sector careers. The Washington Management Services streamlined the personnel system for the state's 2,500 plus middle-level managers. These positions retain the protections of the civil service system but are covered by a separate set of personnel rules that emphasize flexibility, decentralization, and individual accountability. The Executive Search Services effectively designs and carries out a proven method for identifying, screening, interviewing, and ultimately hiring top-level executives for state government.

■ **Window on State Government (BBS)**
State of Texas (EXSL 1994)

The Texas state comptroller's Window on State Government bulletin board system (BBS) was developed by the Comptroller's Research and Application Systems Divisions in an effort to distribute data and information more widely to citizens of the state. Some of the information available to citizens includes: gross and retail sales by city, county, and metro area; employment data by region and metro area; Texas economic indicators; Texas population forecast; local allocation data by city; state spending by category and year; and state revenue by source.

■ Zero Incarceration Placement Program
Los Angeles County, California (EXSL 1992)

An "empowered" Los Angeles County Probation Department work
team implemented an interim foster care placement program that reduces
Juvenile Hall time from 28 to 7 calendar days, and requires no additional
resources. This public-private partnership is operated by three highly
skilled placement deputies who work in concert with the courts and the
various group homes to make the best possible match between minors
and the facilities providing an interim program. The program saves $1.7
million annually in Juvenile Hall costs.

Index

■

About the Authors

—■

Marc Holzer (M.P.A., Ph.D. University of Michigan, Political Science) is Professor of Public Administration at Rutgers University, Campus at Newark, and also serves as Director of the doctoral program in Public Administration and as Executive Director of the National Center for Public Productivity. He is the author or editor of more than a dozen volumes, and has been published widely in professional journals, compendia, and symposia. He has long served as the Editor-in-Chief of *Public Productivity and Management Review,* and his work has been translated into several languages, including Russian.

Kathe Callahan (M.P.A. Rutgers University) is a doctoral student in Public Administration at Rutgers, the State University of New Jersey-Campus at Newark, specializing in public sector productivity. As an Associate Director of the National Center for Public Productivity (NCPP), she is currently leading a 3-year project to involve citizens in the establishment of performance measures in local government. Prior to her doctoral studies, she coordinated the Exemplary State and Local Awards program for the National Center.